Anonymus

Commissioners of Public Works (Ireland)

Fifty-ninth report with appendices

Anonymus

Commissioners of Public Works (Ireland)
Fifty-ninth report with appendices

ISBN/EAN: 9783742811127

Manufactured in Europe, USA, Canada, Australia, Japa

Cover: Foto ©Suzi / pixelio.de

Manufactured and distributed by brebook publishing software
(www.brebook.com)

Anonymus

Commissioners of Public Works (Ireland)

PUBLIC WORKS, IRELAND.

FIFTY-NINTH ANNUAL REPORT

OF THE

COMMISSIONERS OF PUBLIC WORKS

IN

IRELAND:

WITH

APPENDICES,

FOR THE YEAR 1890-91.

Presented to both Houses of Parliament by Command of Her Majesty.

DUBLIN:
PRINTED FOR HER MAJESTY'S STATIONERY OFFICE
BY
ALEXANDER THOM & CO. (LIMITED), ABBEY-STREET,

And to be purchased, either directly or through any Bookseller, from
Hodges, Figgis, and Co., 104, Grafton-street, Dublin.; or
Eyre and Spottiswoode, East Harding-street, Fleet-street, E.C.; or
John Menzies and Co., 12, Hanover-street, Edinburgh, and 66 & 90, West Nile-street, Glasgow.

1891.

TABLE OF CONTENTS.

REPORT AND APPENDICES.

APPENDICES.

PUBLIC WORKS, IRELAND.

FIFTY-NINTH ANNUAL REPORT
— OF THE —

COMMISSIONERS OF PUBLIC WORKS IN IRELAND,
FOR THE YEAR 1890-91.

TO THE LORDS COMMISSIONERS OF HER MAJESTY'S TREASURY.

MAY IT PLEASE YOUR LORDSHIPS,

WE have the honour to submit our Fifty-ninth Annual Report on the several LOANS VOTED, LIGHT RAILWAY, and MISCELLANEOUS services entrusted to our management, viz. :—

I. LOANS :
  (1). Loans secured on Undertakings, e.g. :—
    For Inland Navigation, Harbours, Railways, &c., under 1 & 2 Wm. IV., c. 33.
    For Labourers' Dwellings in Towns, and Housing of Working Classes, under Acts of 1866 and 1883.
  (2). Loans secured on Rates, e.g. :—
    To Grand Juries for Roads, Bridges, Piers, and Harbours, Lunatic Asylum Buildings, Courthouses, Reformatories, and Industrial Schools.
    For purposes sanctioned by the Public Health Acts.
    For Labourers' Dwellings under the Act of 1883.
    For Dispensary Houses.
  (3). Loans secured on Lands, e.g. :—
    For Arterial Drainage Works.
    For Arterial Drainage Maintenance.
    To Owners for improvement of Lands, viz. :—Drainage, erection of Farm Houses and Buildings, of Dwellings for Agricultural Labourers ; Planting for Shelter (10 Vic., c. 32, &c.)
    To Tenants for improvement of their Holdings, viz. :—Drainage, and most of the purposes included in the previous service (44 & 45 Vic., c. 49).
    For Purchase under Land Act, 1870.
  (4). Miscellaneous Loans, e.g. :—
    Glebe Loans.
    For National School Teachers' Residences.
    For Relief of Distress under Act of 1880.
    For Seed Supply under Act of 1890.

II. VOTED SERVICES :
  Public Buildings, Ireland, viz. :—
    Naval and Military ; State and Official Residences ; Civil Departments ; Legal Departments ; Metropolitan Police ; Royal Irish Constabulary ; Dundrum Criminal Lunatic Asylum ; Science and Art Department ; Public Education ; Royal University and Queen's Colleges ; Revenue Departments.
  Royal Parks and Gardens :—
    Phoenix Park ; St. Stephen's-green ; The Curragh of Kildare.
  Royal Harbours :—
    Kingstown ; Howth ; Dunmore ; Ardglass.
  Inland Navigations :—
    Boyne ; Maigue.
  Royal University of Ireland Buildings.
  Science and Art Buildings. New Museum and National Library. Royal Botanic Gardens, Glasnevin.
  Ancient Monuments Protection Act, 45 & 46 Vic., c. 73.

III. NON-VOTED SERVICES :

Arterial Drainage Works.	Irish Reproductive Loan Fund.
Arterial Drainage, Maintenance and Increased Banks, and Railway Clauses Consolidation Act.	Sea and Coast Fisheries (Ireland) Loan Fund.
	National Monuments and Ecclesiastical

The following is an ABSTRACT of LOANS made by the COMMISSIONERS of PUBLIC WORKS, showing the Amounts Remitted, and

No.	Acts under which advances have been made.	PURPOSES FOR WHICH APPLIED.	No. of Loans granted on this Head, 1891.	Advances to Borrowers.		Principal.
				In the Year ended 31st March, 1891.	Total up to the 31st March, 1891.	In the Year ended
						Remitted.
		I. Public Works Loans, 1 & 2 Wm. IV., c. 33, and 40 & 41 Vic., c. 27.				
		CLASS I.—Loans secured on Undertakings.		£ s. d.	£ s. d.	£ s. d.
1	1 & 2 Wm. IV., c. 33.	Local Boards—various works,	39	1,830 0 0	423,634 0 0	34,400 14 10
2	Do.	Inland Navigation, ...	4	14,000 0 0	126,597 0 2	1,883 19 6
3	Do.	Railways, ...	23	—	1,144,707 5 6	45,597 0 6
4	Do.	Quarries, Mines, &c., . .	1	—	18,300 0 0	300 6 6
5	Do.	Harbours, Docks, &c., . .	24	6,500 0 0	216,488 1 9	7,790 10 5
6	Do.	Reclamation of Waste Lands, .	1	—	198,481 0 0	—
7	29 & 30 Vic., c. 44.	Labourers' Dwellings in Towns, .	46	—	148,547 15 6	4,354 6 10

Advances and Repayments in the Year, the Total Advances and Repayments to the 31st March, 1891, the the Balances Outstanding.

ABSTRACT of LOANS made by the Commissioners of Public Works, showing the
Amounts remitted, and

PURPOSES FOR WHICH ADVANCED.	No. of Loans Advanced in the Month, &c.	Amounts so Remitted.		PRINCIPAL In the Year ended
		In the Year ended 31st March, 1891.	Total up to the 31st March, 1891.	Principal
		£ s. d.	£ s. d.	£ s. d.
CLASS III.—continued.				
Improvement of Lands—viz., Drainage, Erection of Farm Buildings and Farm Labourers' Dwellings, Planting for Shelter,	5,070	20,745 0 0	4,067,122 0 14	62,551 7 0
Land Improvement Preliminary Expenses,	1	1,000 0 0	68,469 0 0	800 16 3
Land Law.—Advances to Tenants for Improvement of their Holdings,	6,180	63,000 0 0	728,944 0 0	20,441 6 11
For Advances to Tenants for Purchase of their Holdings, &c.	689	—	318,693 15 7	4,769 11 0

Advances and Repayments in the Year, the Total Advances and Repayments to the 31st March, 1891, and the Balance Outstanding—*continued.*

I.—PUBLIC WORKS LOANS.

In the year ending 31st March, 1891, we have, with the approval of the Lords Commissioners of Her Majesty's Treasury, made 1,147 loans for £687,163, as against 1,065 loans for £424,800, in the previous year. The increase of 82 in the number of loans, and of £262,368 in the amount, is attributable to applications for loans under the Seed Potatoes Supply Act, 1890.

The following statement shows the different purposes for which loans have been made during the year :—

Total Number of Loans for each Class	PURPOSES OF LOANS SANCTIONED FOR—	No.	Amount.	Total Amount for each Class
			£	£
	CLASS I.—LOANS SECURED ON UNDERTAKINGS.			
	Inland Navigation,	1	15,000	
	Harbours,	1	5,000	
28	Labourers' Dwellings,	80	43,413	61,413
	CLASS II.—LOANS SECURED ON RATES.			
	Grand Juries of Counties,	1	900	
	Industrial Schools,	3	6,500	
	Repairs of Post Roads,	1	1,000	
	„ Fishery Piers,	6	784	
	Lunatic Asylums Buildings,	9	13,850	
	Public Health Acts,	80	74,707	
229	Labourers Acts,	128	106,487	
	Dispensary Houses,	23	15,690	219,188
	CLASS III.—LOANS SECURED ON LANDS.			
	River Drainage, 26 & 27 Vic., c. 88,	2	50,006	
	„ Maintenance,	1	930	
	Land Improvement,	141	33,096	
	„ Preliminary Expenses,	1	3,000	
	Land Law Act, 1881, Sec. 19, Labourers' Cottages,	6	445	
680	„ „ Sec. 31, Loans to Tenants for Land Improvement.	529	47,895	109,888
	CLASS IV.—MISCELLANEOUS LOANS.			
	Glebe Loans,	47	80,996	
	National Schools, Teachers' Residences,	54	12,800	
	„ „ and Training Colleges,	2	3,770	
916	Seed Supply Act, 1890,	106	291,542	291,863
1,147				£257,163

OBSERVATIONS ON CLASS (I).—LOANS SECURED ON UNDERTAKINGS.

Loans of this class have, for some years past, shown a tendency to diminish. The amount for which loans were entered into in 1890-91 is £61,413, as against £69,678

wholly depended on the completion of the channel and the obtaining of the certificate of the County Court Judge to that effect before the 31st July, 1891. We are glad to state that this certificate was granted on the 1st January last, and that the Company is now enabled to levy the increased dues.

(2.) Three thousand pounds to the Moy River Harbour Commissioners, on account of an estimated requirement of £9,000, for the purpose of enabling them to deepen the river by dredging, with the object of admitting vessels having a greater draft than twelve feet, the present limit at high water spring tides, to proceed over the bar and up the river to Ballina.

Labourers' Dwellings in Towns and Housing of the Working Classes. Nos. 7 and 8 in Abstract.

29 & 30 Vic., c. 44, 1866 ; and the Housing of the Working Classes Act, 1885, 48 & 49 Vic., c. 72.

Since the passing of the first Act above referred to, in 1866, to the close of the year 1884-85, a period of nineteen years, loans have been sanctioned under the provisions of that and the amending Acts, amounting to £231,334, for the erection of dwellings for 5,416 families, the rate of interest charged being 4 per cent.

The more favourable terms granted by your Lordships' Minute of 23rd January, 1886, as to the rate of interest on such loans, has had the effect of stimulating in some degree those desirous of providing improved dwellings for the labouring classes, and it will be observed that during the year 1888-89 twenty-six loans were made, to the amount of £58,753, for building 573 dwellings, while during the past year applications have been received for loans amounting to £94,766, of which twenty, to the amount of £48,418, have been sanctioned for 532 dwellings.

The following abstract, No. 1, shows the number and amount of the loans made each year during the periods referred to. For observations on The Housing of the Working Classes Act, 1890, see page 19.

Abstract No. 1.

Year.	No. of applications sanctioned.	Amount sanctioned.	No. of families to be accommodated.
		£ s.	
1866-67.	Nil		Nil
1867-68.	1	525 0	6
1868-69.	Nil		Nil
1869-70.	1	500 0	10
1870-71.	1	4,146 0	105
1871-72.	3	1,650 0	18
1872-73.	3	7,175 0	105
1873-74.	7	22,360 0	381
1874-75.	1	910 0	18
1875-76.	7	34,942 0	348
1876-77.	8	11,100 0	128
1877-78.	8	22,514 0	373
1878-79.	10	7,100 0	41
1879-80.	19	31,855 0	551
1880-81.	17	22,570 0	502
1881-82.	17	31,574 0	445
1882-83.	15	21,187 0	270
1883-84.	16	40,083 0	397
1884-85.	18	24,386 0	288
1885-86.	20	52,755 0	715
1886-87.	24	78,151 0	854
1887-88.	80	54,745 10	597
1888-89.	38	53,753 10	573
1889-90.	16	46,319 0	387
1890-91.	20	45,113 0	532
Total.	370	588,681 0	7,184

OBSERVATIONS ON CLASS (2).—LOANS SECURED ON RATES.

The amount for which these loans have been entered into and the number of such loans, show a falling off.

—	1890-91.	1889-91.
Number of Loans, . .	287	229
Amount of Loans, . .	£794,553	£919,152

Loans for Works carried out by Grand Juries. Nos. 9 and 10 in Abstract.

Loans for works, when carried out by Grand Juries, have fallen from £8,200 in 1889-90 to £600 in 1890-91.

Loans for Industrial Schools. No. 11 in Abstract.

Loans for Industrial Schools stand at £6,500 as against £500 for 1889-90.

Loans for Lunatic Asylum Buildings. No. 17 in Abstract.

Nine loans, amounting to £15,850, for additions, &c., to Lunatic Asylum buildings, were entered into as against 12, amounting to £64,925, in the previous year.

Loans under the Public Health Act. No. 19 in Abstract.

Loans under the Public Health Act of 1878 reached in number 50, in amount £74,707, as against the corresponding figures 48 and £57,800 for the previous year. The following table contrasts the two years in detail, and shows some of the many undertakings comprised under the title of "Sanitary Loans."

PURPOSE	1889-90.		1890-91.	
	Number of Loans.	Amount.	Number of Loans.	Amount.
		£		£
Water Works, ...	22	43,695	13	31,850
Sewerage, ...	11	8,720	14	10,077
Burial Grounds, ...	3	3,110	6	3,000
Footpaths, ...	4	1,376	—	—
Municipal Buildings, ...	2	2,900	8	5,740
People's Parks, ...	2	4,600	—	—
Fever Hospital, ...	1	1,000	—	—
Gas Works, ...	—	—	6	5,050
Paving, ...	—	—	1	13,780
Fire Brigade Stations, ...	—	—	—	—
Stabling, Disinfecting Chambers, &c.	—	—	6	5,320
	48	£57,800	50	£74,707

The total amount of Loans authorized for Sanitary purposes stood at £1,747,921 on 31st March, 1891.

The distribution of this sum between different sanitary purposes is as follows :—

	£
Water Works, ...	856,569
Sewerage, ...	619,607
Streets (Paving, &c.), . .	369,374
Public Baths, ...	15,350
Scavenging, ...	79,915
Buildings, Cemeteries, Parks, &c.,	186,406
	£1,747,921

Loans under Labourers Acts. No. 22 in Abstract.

Loans under the Labourers Acts, 1883 and 1885, show an increase in amount on 1889-90, although they are still far below previous years.

1887-88,	.	.	.	. £446,881
1888-89,	.	.	.	. £188,748
1889-90,	.	.	.	. £89,593
1890-91,	.	.	.	. £106,437

The loans sanctioned under these Acts amounted at the end of the year under report to £1,205,849. Ninety-one out of 161 Unions had borrowed this sum. The remaining Unions had not up to that date availed themselves of the powers given by the Acts. The number of Unions which had borrowed, with the amount lent in each province, appears from the following figures:—

				£
Munster,	.	44 Unions,	.	735,844
Leinster,	.	37 „	.	455,481
Connaught,	.	7 „	.	7,519
Ulster,	.	3 „	.	6,005
		91		£1,205,849

The advances under the Acts in 1890-91 amounted to £139,185, bringing the total advanced to £289,024.

Loans for Dispensary Houses. No. 23 in Abstract.

Loans for the construction, &c., of Dispensary Houses have risen from 11 loans for £7,115 in 1889-90, to 28 for £13,860 in 1890-91.

Loans for Public Libraries.

(40 & 41 Vic., cc. 15 & 54.)

No application has been received for advances under these Acts.

OBSERVATIONS ON CLASS (8).—LOANS SECURED ON LANDS.

This class comprises, in addition to loans made to tenants for purchase of their holdings, in accordance with the provisions of the Land Act of 1870 (under which no advances are now made), the following loans, having for their object the improvement of land:—

(a.) Loans for arterial drainage under 5 & 6 Vic., c. 89.
(b.) Loans made for arterial drainage works (26 & 27 Vic., c. 88), and loans made for the maintenance of such works (29 & 30 Vic., c. 49).
(c.) Loans to "owners" of lands for improvements, under 10 Vic., c. 32, and amending Acts.
(d.) Loans to tenants of lands for improvements, under sec. 51 of the Land Law Act, 1881, 44 & 45 Vic., c. 49.

Loans for Arterial Drainage. No. 24 in Abstract.

Loans for Arterial Drainage were made from 1842 to 1862 under 5 and 6 Vic., c. 89. £2,082,032 were lent under this statute, the greater part during and after the famine of 1849. Of this amount £1,207,583 was remitted, and £373,837 principal (with £788,104 interest), repaid. The principal still repayable amounts to £682.

Loans for Arterial Drainage, under 26 and 27 Vic., c. 88, were made in three cases to the aggregate amount of £30,005.

Owners who are not occupiers have for some time past ceased generally to initiate Arterial Drainage undertakings, and as tenants have no statutory power to do so, loans for this purpose are now seldom made.

The entire amount of loans entered into for these purposes up to March 31, 1891, is £824,877, including £6,135 lent out of the Irish Church Fund. Of this amount, £814,787 had by that date been advanced, of which £14,195 was advanced in the year under report.

Further information as to Arterial Drainage will be found at page 35.

Loans for Land Improvement.   No. 27 in Abstract

...of the Board's duties we beg to submit, as usual, the numbers of ...ams, and the amounts issued in each year from the commencement to ...f the financial year, 31st March, 1891 :—

No. of Applications	Amount Issued				No. of Applications	Amount Issued
1,364	£72,790	1870–71,	.	.	158	£77,88
673	216,160	1871–72,	.	.	160	89,46
643	376,838	1872–73,	.	.	173	78,55
488	250,324	1873–74,	.	.	234	99,57
380	145,665	1874–75,	.	.	245	103,60
164	85,543	1875–76,	.	.	264	86,73
134	55,484	1876–77,	.	.	311	151,48
185	49,235	1877–78,	.	.	379	121,34
89	35,160	1878–79,	.	.	413	136,35
108	34,510	1879–80, { Relief, 2,144		3,607	724,81
314	31,574	{ Ordinary, 463 }			
119	35,634	1880–81,	.	.	638	766,68
111	39,334	1881–82,	.	.	401	290,88
138	74,908	1882–83,	.	.	481	135,83
134	36,655	1883–84,	.	.	503	122,06
164	41,278	1884–85,	.	.	394	117,60
135	66,550	1885–86,	.	.	378	79,67
133	56,430	1886–87,	.	.	719	63,19
90	45,210	1887–88,	.	.	151	45,78
96	73,335	1888–89,	.	.	148	30,79
143	59,150	1889–90,	.	.	188	34,67
170	46,773	1890–81,	.	.	213	39,76

The following table gives the number of loans and the sums issued in the several counties of Ireland up to the 31st March, 1891 :—

SCHEDULE showing the NUMBER of LOANS and AMOUNTS ISSUED from commencement of ACT.

Name of County.	No. of Loans.	Amount issued.	Total No. of Loans	Total Amount issued.
		£ s. d.		£ s. d.
NORTHERN DIVISION.				
Antrim, ...	199	152,498 0 0		
Londonderry, . . .	144	66,843 0 0		
Donegal	252	187,571 0 0		
Fermanagh, . . .	166	82,489 0 0		
Tyrone, ...	207	144,735 0 0		
Armagh, ...	64	81,713 0 0		
Down, ...	142	93,481 0 0	1,326	723,879 0 0
MIDLAND AND EASTERN.				
Cavan, ...	164	83,817 0 0		
Monaghan, . . .	84	63,841 0 0		
Longford, . . .	317	177,991 0 0		
Louth, ...	89	57,904 0 0		
Meath, ...	403	185,631 0 0		
Westmeath, . . .	253	93,940 0 0		
Dublin, ...	245	65,363 0 0		
Kildare, ...	378	144,772 0 0		
King's, ...	204	81,035 0 0		
Queen's, ...	315	151,233 0 0		
Wicklow, ...	253	120,441 0 0		
Carlow, ...	311	105,749 0 0		
Kilkenny, . . .	176	66,931 0 0		
Wexford, ...	289	155,921 0 0	3,304	1,493,573 0 0
WESTERN.				
Sligo, ...	253	135,807 0 0		
Leitrim, ...	197	74,450 0 0		
Mayo, ...	601	337,575 0 0		
Roscommon, . . .	453	537,028 0 0		
Galway, ...	770	381,153 0 0		
Clare, ...	460	144,993 0 0	2,843	1,511,006 0 0
SOUTHERN.				
Limerick, ...	743	378,034 0 0		
Tipperary, . . .	580	503,929 0 0		
Waterford, . . .	167	66,580 0 0		
Cork, ...	1,283	651,651 0 0		
Kerry, ...	784	165,769 0 0	3,499	1,533,913 0 0
		Totals, . .	10,766	£4,930,181 0 0

MAIN AND THOROUGH DRAINAGE.

The number of loans sanctioned for works, of which thorough drainage forms the principal part, since the commencement in 1847 to the 31st March in this year, is 9,198, for £3,697,852, and of this number 86, for £10,025, were approved during the year ended 31st March, 1891.

PLANTING FOR SHELTER.

Since the passing of the Act 29 and 30 Vic., c. 40, 114 loans, amounting to £23,905, have been made, and of that number 6, for £1,335, were sanctioned during the year now reported on.

FARM BUILDINGS.

Under this head 9,588 loans have been sanctioned since the passing of the Act 13 and 14 Vic., c. 19, the amount being £1,102,661. This includes 82 loans, for £20,963, approved during the past financial year.

DWELLINGS FOR AGRICULTURAL LABOURERS.

For this class of work the number of loans sanctioned since the passing of the Act 23 Vic., c. 19, is 692, for £383,380, 17 of which, amounting to £4,865, were approved since our last Report.

Loans to Tenants for Improvement of Holdings.　No. 29 in Abstract.

LAND LAW (IRELAND) ACT, 1881.

Sections 19 and 31.

Under section 19 of the above quoted Act we have power to make advances to tenant farmers, who, pursuant to the injunctions of the Irish Land Commission, and as a condition attached to the fixing of a "fair rent," proceed to erect labourers' dwellings on their holdings. Six loans were sanctioned, amounting to £466, under this section within the year ending 31st March, 1891, the amount issued being £991. Under this provision of the Act 253 loans have been sanctioned since the commencement, amounting to £14,876, the instalments issued amounting to £13,346.

Under section 31 of the same Act, which provides for loans to occupying tenants for improvements proposed by themselves, the number of loans sanctioned since our last report was 528, amounting to £47,395, the sum issued being £43,860. This gives the total of loans sanctioned under section 31 since the commencement to 31st March, 1891, as 10,208—amount £872,767, the instalments issued amounting to £723,944.

The number of applications for loans lodged during the year 1890-91 was 767.

The above shows an increase, both in the number of loans sanctioned and the amount issued.

The reports of the Local Inspectors bear testimony to the increased prosperity and industry of the borrowers, and to the satisfactory manner in which they execute the work. They also notice a great spirit of improvement in those tenants who have acquired the ownership of their farms under the provisions of the Land Purchase Acts.

The following table gives the distribution by Counties of the sums issued for all classes of work under the 31st Section of the Land Law (Ireland) Act, 1881 :—

SCHEDULE showing the NUMBER of LOANS SANCTIONED and AMOUNTS ISSUED up to the 31st MARCH, 1891.

PROVINCES AND COUNTIES.	Number of Loans Sanctioned.			Amount Sanctioned.			Total Issues.		
	To 1st Mar., 1890.	Year ending 31st Mar., 1891.	Total Number.	1st Mar., 1890.	Year ending 31st Mar., 1891.	Total Sanctioned.	To 31st Mar., 1890.	Year ending 31st Mar., 1891.	Total Issues.
LEINSTER:				£	£	£	£	£	£
Carlow,	58	3	61	7,7M	483	8,250	8,084	564	8,468
Dublin,	69	8	77	11,160	740	11,880	9,083	1,314	10,430
Kildare,	112	7	119	18,110	1,718	19,831	13,740	2,858	18,948
Kilkenny,	94	6	100	8,726	850	10,588	7,138	448	7,646
King's,	170	20	190	15,843	1,794	17,690	13,810	728	13,544
Longford,	263	7	270	23,724	620	24,414	20,184	640	20,785
Louth,	25	6	41	4,446	1,188	4,740	8,862	895	4,787
Meath,	112	16	128	19,838	1,929	31,760	14,084	3,137	18,181
Queen's,	78	11	67	7,495	1,103	8,683	8,935	364	4,990
Westmeath,	211	13	224	88,840	981	24,821	18,198	8,167	10,383
Wexford,	88	12	100	8,643	860	9,823	7,888	852	8,140
Wicklow,	85	18	97	9,695	990	10,683	7,741	871	8,618
Totals,	1,571	116	1,697	190,870	13,165	173,185	127,170	12,134	140,604
MUNSTER:									
Clare,	614	16	832	20,548	1,718	59,560	18,543	1,030	44,873
Cork,	1,673	78	1,750	144,339	6,789	151,118	124,834	7,708	130,533
Kerry,	656	43	679	51,170	3,078	54,943	39,357	2,064	41,581
Limerick,	477	20	507	47,610	3,000	50,610	57,440	3,430	51,050
Tipperary,	363	43	408	34,618	4,050	38,688	27,801	1,548	81,188
Waterford,	48	3	50	4,530	125	9,655	4,000	851	4,334
Totals,	4,530	214	4,044	333,910	18,780	361,870	274,128	17,849	293,007
ULSTER:									
Antrim,	88	14	107	8,910	1,670	10,680	7,484	1,057	8,511
Armagh,	75	1	78	4,930	60	4,970	8,987	60	4,041
Cavan,	596	15	619	40,148	1,000	41,148	83,849	881	34,740
Donegal,	137	16	243	16,485	1,385	17,847	8,328	1,140	9,417
Down,	62	11	62	4,845	1,045	6,340	13,884	771	14,634
Fermanagh,	187	9	186	8,650	470	9,180	6,788	464	7,242
Londonderry,	101	11	113	7,800	1,180	8,780	6,819	1,000	7,653
Monaghan,	88	16	80	6,078	1,458	8,600	3,013	424	8,448
Tyrone,	218	10	229	17,638	625	18,350	14,845	718	14,573
Totals,	1,843	101	1,644	114,728	8,860	123,A43	94,788	8,884	101,834
CONNAUGHT:									
Galway,	650	20	570	44,780	1,788	48,805	89,108	1,571	40,370
Leitrim,	571	11	482	36,918	875	36,790	31,526	620	32,446
Mayo,	940	7	941	38,448	418	69,680	60,618	884	61,274
Roscommon,	434	20	467	53,445	3,454	56,100	37,339	2,673	38,413
Sligo,	438	16	443	33,808	1,250	34,385	28,693	1,448	30,134
Totals,	3,921	67	3,008	215,780	6,880	223,390	188,016	5,991	194,009
Grand Totals,	9,678	528	10,803	855,878	47,895	872,187	685,084	48,860	729,044

We also beg to submit a statement classifying the loans in which works have been completed under the different descriptions of work, to the 31st March, 1890 :—

Description of Work.	Amount Expended.		
	From granting of Act or end of March, 1890.	For year ending 31st March, 1891.	Total from granting of Act to 31st March, 1891.
	£ s. d.	£ s. d.	£ s. d.
Drainage, Fencing, Farm Roads, and other Land Works,	354,378 12 5	10,681 14 1	364,060 7 6
Farm Houses and Offices,	297,854 11 4	27,840 14 0	320,495 5 4
Labourers' Cottages, 19th section,	9,776 10 10	551 0 0	0,327 10 10
Labourers' Cottages, 31st section,	6,877 10 5	1,168 14 8	1,855 5 1
Scutch Mills for Flax,	500 0 3	— — —	500 0 3
	663,856 8 4	42,940 8 7	708,476 8 11

The number of loans in which the amounts sanctioned have been expended, and the works certified as completed, is 6,324, and those in which the works were still in progress on the 31st March, 1891, were 757.

OBSERVATIONS ON CLASS (4).—MISCELLANEOUS LOANS.

Globe Loans. No. 81 in Abstract.

Fifty-two applications for loans have been received during the year, amounting to £39,688, and 47 loans have been granted for £30,950. The issues for the year have amounted to £30,412. Since passing of the first Act, 1876, we have received 1,859 applications, of which the following is an abstract of those on which loans were made to 31st March, 1891.

—	No.	Amount.
		£
Church of Ireland,	245	128,389
Roman Catholic,	854	257,658
Presbyterian,	709	63,595
Wesleyan and other,	69	90,007
	1,877	488,623

Loans for building Schools and Training Colleges. No. 86 in Abstract.

Loans for building and improving non-vested schools and training colleges have increased from £1,981, in 1889-90, to £2,770.

Loans for National School Teachers' Residences. No. 85 in Abstract.

The demand for loans for National school teachers' residences, which showed a continuous increase up to 1889-90, has fallen for the past year from 70 loans of £15,430 in the former, to 54 loans of £12,400 in the latter year. The total advances for these loans up to 31st March, 1891, was £118,781.

Loans under Seed Potatoes Supply Act, 1890. No. 34 in Abstract.

Loans, to the amount £261,542, have been made under Seed Potatoes Supply (Ireland) Act, 1890, the provisions of which are explained in a subsequent paragraph. Full details as to the extent to which different localities were aided by these Loans will be found in Appendix E and in the Map annexed.

IRISH CHURCH FUND LOANS.

LEGISLATION OF 1890 AFFECTING THE LOAN SERVICE.

The Seed Potatoes Supply (Ireland) Act, 1890, was passed in order to provide seed potatoes for localities unable, through poverty, and the failure of the potato crop, to procure from ordinary resources an adequate supply. It enabled Boards of Guardians to apply to the Local Government Board, on behalf of each Electoral Division requiring assistance, and empowered the Board of Works, on receipt of such applications approved of by the Local Government Board, to make loans on the security of the Poor Rate leviable in the Electoral Division aided. The loans are repayable by two instalments, on the 1st August, 1892 and 1893. The interest which is fixed at the lowest rate accepted by the Treasury on local loans in Ireland (3½ per cent.), is payable out of the Irish Church Fund. The Guardians are entrusted with the duties of selling the seed to occupiers, and of recovering the price from them. The Lord Lieutenant is given power, on application of the Guardians, to postpone to a date, not later than August 1st, 1895, the payment of (1) instalments of loans due by the Guardians to the Board of Works; (2) instalments of price due by purchasers to the Guardians.

The Glebe Loans (Ireland) Act has been continued to December 31st, 1891. The Public Works Loans Act, 1890, enabled the National Debt Commissioners to issue for loans in Ireland any sums not exceeding in the whole £1,000,000. It wrote off, as "Losses on Local Loans" in accordance with the 15th section of the National Debt and Local Loans Act, 1887, £921 7s., composed of sums lent for the different purposes set forth in the first column of the following table:—

Purpose of Advance.	Act Authorizing Advance.	Amount Advanced.	Amount Repaid.	Amount Outstanding.	Amount to be written off applied out of Local Loan Fund.
		£ s. d.	£ s. d.	£ s. d.	£ s. d.
Improvement of Landed Property.	10 Vic., s. 32	350 0 0	47 9 6	302 10 6	302 10 6
Artificial Drainage.	26 & 27 Vic., c. 88.	1,805 15 10	124 9 2	1,181 6 8	64 9 7
Improvement of Holdings.	14 & 15 Vic., c. 49, c. 81.	655 0 0	60 9 6	594 10 6	554 7 11
		2,310 15 10	232 8 0	2,078 7 10	921 7 0

It likewise extinguished arrears, amounting to £344 14s. 2d. principal, and £14 16s. 4d. interest, due in respect of a loan to the Grand Jury of Galway county for the repair of Killeany Pier.

The Housing of the Working Classes Act, 1890, repeals the Labouring Classes Dwellings Act, 1866, and the greater part of the Housing of the Working Classes Act, 1885. The third part of the Act enables us to make loans to Urban Sanitary Authorities, to certain Companies, to owners of lands in fee-simple or under leases, with at least fifty years unexpired, in order to provide dwellings for workmen, to which, in certain cases, a garden may be attached, to alter and improve existing buildings, to provide suitable fixtures and conveniences, and in certain cases, to purchase lands for building workmen's houses. Interest on such loans, varying with the term of repayment, will range from 3¼ to 5½ per cent.

ADVANCES, REPAYMENTS, AND ARREARS.

The earliest mention of Public Works Loans to be found in the Abstract submitted by the Board is in connection with the Statute 57 Geo. III., c. 34, passed in 1817. The total of all loan advances from that date to 31st March, 1891 (with certain loans made under special Acts before 1817), is £38,603,597.

The classified abstract at pages 6-9, shows how this amount has been disposed of by repayments, remissions, balances outstanding, &c.

		£
Total Repayments,	. . . .	21,995,388
Total Remissions,	. . . .	7,914,874
Written off from Local Loan Fund,	. .	59,548
Outstanding Balances,	. . . .	8,573,213
		38,503,567

This outstanding balance is represented in the books of the Office by 23,078 open accounts, which are generally in course of repayment by half-yearly instalments.

The advances to borrowers in the years 1890-91 out of moneys advanced by the National Debt Commissioners were £691,085, as against £477,406 in 1889-90, and £557,022 in 1888-89.

The amounts received in the year were £668,502, in repayment of principal, and £253,495 in respect of interest, making together £921,997. Of the latter amount, £870,007 was paid to the National Debt Commissioners, and £51,990 to the Irish Land Commission, in discharge of principal and interest of loans made out of the Irish Church Fund.

The following table shows the payments, and the arrears of principal and interest for the last four years:—

—	Payments.	Arrears of Principal and Interest.
	£	£
1887-88,	596,021	426,019
1888-89,	762,840	430,338
1889-90,	748,942	465,718
1890-91,	921,997	503,790

The following Abstract shows the services on which these arrears occur :—

—	31st March, 1888.	31st March, 1889.	31st March, 1890.	31st March, 1891.
	£	£	£	£
Public Works Loans generally,	16,752	21,773	23,376	24,274
Clare Slob Reclamation Loan,	17,412	13,371	28,567	33,443
Public Health Act,	2,997	7,333	3,767	2,310
Railways,	249,338	289,916	309,481	345,383
Land Charges, payable by Owners,	91,672	86,658	77,179	73,189
Do., do. Occupiers,	3,461	4,476	5,538	7,345
Seed Supply,	34,957	79,884	17,002	14,916
	426,019	438,338	465,318	503,790

The loans under the Public Health Act, those to land owners and to land occupiers for improvement, and the Seed Supply loans, show a decrease in arrears. Those for Public Works generally show a slight increase. A year's interest has been added to the previous arrears of the Clare Slob debt. Loans on Railways continue to be the main cause of increase in arrears. The arrears on this head for the year amount to £88,794.

Land Improvement Arrears, payable by owners, continue to diminish. They stand for 1890-91 at £73,226, as against £77,179 for 1889-90, and they have been lessened by £16,444 in the last three years. Receivers, appointed by the Court on the application of the Department, continue in many instances to collect the rents.

RATES OF INTEREST.

The average rate chargeable on the advances out of the Local Loans Fund was £3 13s. 3d. on the 31st March, 1839; £3 12s. on the 31st March, 1890; and £3 11s. 10d. on the 31st March, 1891. The interest realised in the year averaged £3 6s. 8d. per cent. on the principal sum outstanding on the 1st April, 1890.

VOTED SERVICES.

Under this second head of our duties, comprising those services which are created by, or maintained from, annual votes of Parliament, the accounts detailed in the Appendix (A) record the following expenditure on each to 31st March, 1891, and the second column shows the expenditure on the same votes for the preceding year 1889-90 :—

	1890-91.	1889-90.
Class I.	£	£
Public Works and Buildings, and Railways, Ireland.	328,377	199,568
Science and Art Buildings, Dublin,	—	23,391
Class II.		
Public Works Office,	36,825	37,573
	364,879	260,937

Showing the total charge against the Consolidated Fund for the year to be £365,202. But as from these services we have derived rents, tolls, fees, &c., amounting to £9,914, of which the sum of £9,753 has been paid or will be paid over to Her Majesty's Exchequer in aid of Revenue, the net charge amounts to £355,449.

PUBLIC BUILDINGS.

General Observations.

Royal Hospital.—Considerable progress has been made in the restoration of the roof of portion of this building, the timbers of which were in an advanced state of decay. The new roof over the dining hall has been completed, and that over the Master's quarters is in an advanced state. In addition to renewal of the roof of this portion of the building, it has been necessary to rebuild two of the internal walls which carry the flues, as they were found to be in a defective and dangerous condition, and some of the floors and partitions were in such an unsound state that their immediate renewal was found necessary. These additional works together with other works of a minor character consequent on these extensive restorations, have delayed the completion of the work and have increased its cost considerably.

Preparations are now being made for the renewal of the chapel roof.

Coast Guard Stations.—The new stations at Dingle, Co. Kerry (with residence for the Divisional Officer) and at Barrow-in-Fenit in same county, have been completed. The station at Kells, Co. Kerry, has been improved and a second story added to the building. At Clandeboye, Co. Down, a new boat-house has been erected.

Contracts have been entered into for new stations at Bannow and Carnsore, both in Co. Wexford, and the works are in progress.

Royal Naval Reserve.—Sites for Naval Reserves at Galway and Kinsale have been acquired and that for Belfast is still under consideration.

Ordnance Survey Office.—The apparatus for extinguishing fires has been supplied, and preparations are now being made for the erection of a new map store.

Dublin Metropolitan Police.—Kingstown new court and offices have been completed, and are now being occupied.

Royal Irish Constabulary Barracks.—The new barracks at Browne's-square and Cullingtree-road in Belfast were completed and occupied. Considerable progress made with the barrack at Glenravel-street, and a contract has been entered into for the central barrack. The new barrack at Derrypark, Co. Galway, is well advanced, that at Mullingar has been completed and is now occupied.

The works necessary to convert the cavalry barracks at Athy into a Constabulary barrack have been carried out, and the buildings are now occupied by the police. Banaha barrack, Co. Tipperary, has also been altered and occupied.

Postal and Telegraph Offices.—The erection of new offices at Ennis and Coleraine is in progress. The fittings of the office at Ballinasloe have been completed, and that office is now open to the public.

Negotiations have been carried on for the acquisition of sites for new offices at James's-street, Phibsborough, and for a new depot for Parcel Post in Dublin, and also for new offices at Mallow, Tipperary, Drogheda, and Lisburn.

Botanic Gardens.—The building of the new Library and offices in connection with it have been completed.

National Education Buildings.—Grants in aid of the erection of new schools, and improvement of existing schools, to the amount of £17,381 have been paid, as against £21,169 in 1889-90.

DEPOSITORIES FOR PAROCHIAL RECORDS.

Act 39 & 40 Vic., c. 58.

Under the provisions of this Act, inspections of proposed Depositories have been made in 11 cases, and reports thereon forwarded to the Deputy Keeper of the Records.

PARKS AND GARDENS.

The Phœnix Park.—The several buildings, roads, plantations, &c., have been properly maintained, and the People's Garden continues to be highly appreciated by the public as a place of recreation.

St. Stephen's-green Park has been maintained in good order, which is rendered difficult in some respects in consequence of the great numbers who are attracted to it.

The Curragh of Kildare.—The Deputy Ranger's House has been maintained in good order.

NEW MUSEUM OF SCIENCE AND ART, AND NATIONAL LIBRARY BUILDINGS.

The erection of these buildings, with entrance gates, &c., were completed towards the close of last year, and all necessary fittings, furniture, and cases, have since then been provided.

The collection of the Royal Irish Academy in Dawson-street has been transferred to the rooms in the new Museum set apart for that purpose, and the transfer of the books from the old Library in Leinster House to the new National Library has been completed.

A contract was made in June last for lighting the Museum and National Library buildings by electricity, and the works were sufficiently advanced to admit of the Library being lighted by that means during the last winter. The installation has since then been completed in a very satisfactory manner, and the lighting has with great advantage been extended to the Art Schools.

ROYAL HARBOUR.

KINGSTOWN HARBOUR, Co. DUBLIN.

HOWTH HARBOUR, Co. DUBLIN.

The works have been maintained in good order, including the sea slopes of the East and West Piers. The dredging of the entrance of the Harbour and alongside West Pier was completed, a quantity of 15,831 tons having been dredged and deposited on the slob near the Railway station during the year. The large fishing craft frequenting the harbour can now enter at all times of tide.

For remarks as to trade and fishing, see Appendix B.

DUNMORE HARBOUR, Co. WATERFORD.

Notwithstanding the severe storms experienced at this port last autumn, no damage occurred to the works of the harbour; 500 tons of large blocks have been placed at the foot of the paved sea slope to protect it.

The works have been maintained in good order.

For remarks as to trade and fishing, see Appendix B.

DONAGHADEE HARBOUR, Co. DOWN.

Very trifling damage was done to the sea slopes by the winter's storms, and they are being repaired. Some rock ridges inside the harbour were levelled. The works generally have been kept in good order.

Particulars of the trade and fishing of the port are given in Appendix B.

ARDGLASS HARBOUR, Co. DOWN.

The works at this harbour have been maintained in good order, and no damage worth speaking of has been done by the sea. Considerable improvement has been made by the excavation of rock at the south end of the new harbour, by which good-sized cargo steamers and sailing vessels drawing over twelve feet water have discharged at the additional berth thus made available. For Trade and Fishing, see Appendix B.

SHANNON DRAINAGE.

LOUGH ALLEN.

In consequence of floods the works could not be recommenced till the month of May, 1890. They were then carried on with vigour, but on the 2nd August one of the dams was maliciously cut, flooding the work, and carrying with it fully 1,000 cubic yards of silt, which had to be subsequently re-excavated. The works had to be again suspended owing to floods in October, and it was not till the 16th March last that they could be resumed. The main channel is now finished, and but little remains to be done on this division to complete the work provided for in the estimate.

KILLALOE.

The works on this division were carried on as rapidly as was possible with the limited number of men which could be obtained (varying from 100 to 140), and the suspension of the works during floods. Operations were confined to dredging in the river channel above the sluices, and excavation below them, on the Tipperary side, till stopped by the winter floods. At the bridge, all masonry work has been completed, except what may be necessary in underpinning some of the old arches of the bridge. The river bed consisting of very hard clay with boulders, the excavation work has necessarily proved tedious, and has, from its nature, been only to a small extent used for purposes of relief. As remarked in previous Reports, these works will, on completion, prove of great importance, as affording much greater command over the discharge of the Shannon than has hitherto existed.

SHANNON SLUICES.

The sluices have been worked well, and the absence of complaints shows that they were satisfactory.

There was no flood to signify from February, 1890, till November, when there was a very high flood.

The sluices, especially at Killaloe, were opened or closed during the fishing season only in the evening or very early in the morning, so as to avoid disturbing the water by a sudden rise or fall, and the Board have not heard of any complaint from the fishermen.

Some repairs were required at Tarmonbarry, where there was some scour below the sluices, and some of the planking had to be renewed at different places; the gangway at Killaloe had to be renewed almost entirely.

RIVER MAIGUE NAVIGATION.

The swivel bridge had both the upper and lower sheeting renewed, and the collector's house had small repairs done to it.

The house will have to be nearly re-roofed this coming year, as the timber is in very bad order.

LOWER BOYNE NAVIGATION.

The works have been maintained in good order during the year. An extensive breach in the towing path near Oldbridge was promptly repaired without further injury to the works.

ROYAL UNIVERSITY.

The Board have, under the arrangement sanctioned by their Lordships, maintained this building in good order and repair.

ANCIENT MONUMENTS PROTECTION ACT, 1882.

45 and 46 Vic., c. 73.

The necessary steps have been taken for the preservation of those Ancient Monuments the guardianship of which has, under the provisions of the above Act, been handed over to the Commissioners, and some considerable works of exploration and repair have been carried out at New Grange, in the county Meath.

In June last an Order in Council was made, prescribing that the following monuments, being monuments of a like character to the monuments described in the Schedule to the above Act, shall be deemed to be Ancient Monuments to which the above Act applies—

Monument.	County.	Parish.
Cahermacnaghten and Beehive Structures on the Promontory of Dingle	Kerry,	Drumyola and Ballinvoher.
Round Tower, Lusk,	Dublin,	Rowerds.
Round Tower, Kells,	Meath,	Kells.
Stone Cashel, with Callerica	Sligo,	Coolodaras.
Stone Circles and Pillar Stones,	Fermanagh,	Kealshillan.
Round Tower of Tullaherin,	Kilkenny,	Tullaherin.
Round Tower of Rathmichael, Church and Stone Cross,	Dublin,	Rathmichael.

A general description of the first two monuments, the works necessary for the preservation of which are in progress, will be found in the report of Sir Thomas N. Deane in the Appendix C to this Report.

III.—NON-VOTED SERVICES.

This division of our duties comprises a variety of services placed under our control or management in pursuance of several Acts of Parliament. Though numerous, some of them are of only casual occurrence, and therefore do not form the subject of any maritime counties are applied to the purpose of loans to aid fishermen in buying boats, gear, nets, or in creating oyster beds; and in the case of two inland counties, Roscommon and Tipperary, to works of general utility by any Town Commissioners in these counties.

The Sea and Coast Fisheries Fund, which was handed over to us, in pursuance of an Act passed in 1884, is applicable for Fishery Loans in all the maritime counties of Ireland, a preference being given to those counties which are not in possession of any assignment under the Irish Reproductive Loan Fund.

Another important branch is the care and preservation of 187 National ecclesiastical structures which have been vested in us from time to time, and are maintained out of a grant of £50,000 allocated for the purpose from the Irish Church Fund in pursuance of the Irish Church Act, 1869.

Certain duties in connexion with the Grand Jury system of Ireland still devolve on us, the principal of which are the occasional repair of Post Roads, the examination of County Surveyors' Assistants, the building of bridges between counties, and other miscellaneous duties.

The Report also shows that we are charged with certain duties in connexion with Limited Owners' Residences, Arbitrations under the Railway Acts, and in aiding the Local Government Board with certain financial duties connected with the Public Health Act, and Emigration.

The Commissioners for the general control and correspondence, and for superintending and directing the erection, establishment, and regulation of the Asylums for Lunatic Poor comprise the Chairman of this Board associated with the Inspectors of Lunacy and other gentlemen, and the duties have been carried on as if forming part of the regular duties of this department.

The Board, acting under the powers conferred on them by the 45th, 46th, and 47th sections of the Act 1 & 2 Wm. IV., c. 33, and by deeds of mortgage, have entered into possession of the Letterkenny and Southern Railways, and exercise control over Galway Harbour.

The Annual Accounts in these matters are included under the head of Services.

The receipts and expenditure incurred under the Miscellaneous Services are detailed in the Appendix A 4, A 5, A 6, and A 7, and amount to £114,725 and £109,071 respectively, as against £90,991 and £26,489 in the year to 31st March, 1890.

ARTERIAL DRAINAGE AND IMPROVEMENT OF LANDS (IRELAND) ACT, 1863, AND AMENDMENTS. 26 & 27 Vic., c. 88; 27 & 28 Vic., c. 72; 26 & 29 Vic., c. 52; 59 & 53 Vic., c. 72; 55 & 36 Vic., c. 31; 37 & 38 Vic., c. 32; 41 & 42 Vic., c. 59; and 43 & 44 Vic., c. 27.

The total number of applications received from the passing of the first of these Acts in the year 1863 to the 31st of March, 1890, is ninety-five.

The maps, plans, estimates, and valuation schedules have been deposited, together with petitions for the constitution of the Drainage District of the Suck river, county Cork, and for the Carrigobane, Maglin, and BallinasLig Drainage District, county Cork; but the promoters of the former have not up to the present proceeded further with the matter.

The works have been in progress in the year in the following districts:— River Suck, counties Galway and Roscommon; Ballycollton, county Tipperary; and Hillard River, county Cork; and in the following cases the final awards have been made—Glashean River, county Cork; Greanagh River, county Limerick; Ceabes River, county Kerry; Tramore River, county Cork; Lough and River Erne Drainage and Navigation, counties of Fermanagh, Cavan, Monaghan, and Donegal.

A schedule of the final awards made under these Acts will be found in the Appendix. The total area of land drained or improved in the 53 districts in which final awards have been made, is 93,454 statute acres, and the total cost chargeable thereto amounts to £581,848. This has been in addition to the works of the 131 districts, carried out under the Act 5 & 6 Vic., c. 89, and the Acts amending it, between the years 1842 and 1860, on which an expenditure of £2,890,612 was incurred, of which £70,201 was for works chargeable on counties; £141,073 a free grant; £1,306,313 remitted; and £1,043,927 made repayable by annuity or otherwise; a total of 266,738 acres were drained or improved under the latter Act. The particulars of the Lough Erne Drainage and Navigation Award are included in the above amounts and areas, but the award was not dated until after the close of the financial year.

DRAINAGE MAINTENANCE.

29 & 30 Vic., cap. 49.

There was one case of maintenance, viz, the Nobber District, in the county of Meath, where the works have been completed at a cost of £667 1 s. 6d.

RAILWAY CLAUSES CONSOLIDATION ACT.

8 Vic., c. 20, sec. 25.

In the following cases the certificates of dimensions of culverts and waterways have been issued :—

> Ballinrobe to Claremorris.
> Mitchelstown to Fermoy.
> Bantry to Dunry Pier.

FISHERY PIERS AND HARBOURS MAINTENANCE.

16 & 17 Vic., c. 136.

The Grand Jury of County Donegal having failed to maintain the works handed over to them in three cases, viz., at Bunerana, Bundoran, and Malinbeg, his Excellency the Lord Lieutenant applied for and obtained your Lordships' sanction, under provision of the above-quoted Act. The necessary works have been completed.

The damage at Cleggan, County Galway, referred to in last year's Report, has also been repaired under your Lordships' authority.

SEA FISHERIES (IRELAND) ACT, 1883.

We are now enabled to report to your Lordships that the works mentioned under the above-quoted Act, particulars of which are given at page 66 of our Annual Report, 1889-90, have been completed.

The original estimate for these works, exclusive of engineering and law costs, was £239,258. The actual cost was £233,643, including all storm damages during construction, and extra works of a structural nature, principally due to the necessity for additional masonry and excavation where the foundation to be built on was unsound, showing a gross saving of £5,615, which was expended on works for additional accommodation.

Combining these results with those obtained under the Relief of Distress Act, 1881, particulars of which are given in our Annual Report for 1883-84 (page 26), it will be seen that the construction of 98 works, estimated to cost £313,018, was completed for a sum of £807,475, being a gross saving of £6,543.

The balance of the Sea Fishery Fund unexpended at the close of the last financial year was £5,308, and it is estimated that the repayment of loans during the current year will amount to £2,200, or say £7,500 altogether. Of this sum £4,735 will be required for the completion of the works at Greystones, being the balance of a grant of £7,000 sanctioned for additional works. These latter, consisting of a north groyne to intercept the shingle, are progressing very satisfactorily.

The Map attached shows the position of each pier and harbour according to the number on list, Appendix F.

ARKLOW HARBOUR.

Your Lordships having sanctioned an expenditure of £7,000 on a north groyne (the construction of which formed portion of the original design for the harbour), one-half of this sum to be a free grant voted by Parliament, and the other a loan secured on the rates of the township of Arklow, the Harbour Commissioners submitted a design for the works, differing in some respects from that proposed by the Board. After some consideration, the design finally submitted has been agreed to, and arrangements have been made for the early prosecution of the work by the Harbour Commissioners.

CLARE SLOB RECLAMATION.

The strengthening the embankment at the Island Magrath and was stopped on the 3rd June, 1890, by a strike among the men, and work was not recommenced till about the 20th October, when the boundary fences were begun. These, with the drain to the sluice No. 1, were then made, and subsequently the strengthening the embankment was again proceeded with, haysead being sown, as soon as the season permitted, on the

SHANNON NAVIGATION.

The works of this navigation have been maintained in good order during the year. Considerable repairs were executed along the Limerick Canal, and the shallow places were dredged with the Priestman dredger, borrowed from the drainage works. This work was executed at the very low price of two pence per ton.

The breast gates at Athlone were renewed, and the deep gates at Tarmonbarry also, the old ones at these places having become unsafe. The bridges at Portumna and Tarmonbarry had the sheeting of the roadway renewed.

IRISH REPRODUCTIVE LOAN FUND.

The following statement shows the total amount advanced on loan for fishery purposes (with two exceptions, viz., in counties Roscommon and Tipperary, for the erection of a Town Hall), in each of the ten counties interested, up to 31st December, 1890, the date of the last Parliamentary return, and the total repayments to the same date :—

County.	No. of Loans	Total Amount advanced to 31st December, 1890.	Total Amount to be repaid, including interest at the rate of 2½ per cent. per annum.	Repayments to 31st December, 1890.	Balance available for Loan, being Cash Balances and Consols in credit on 1st January, 1891.
		£ s. d.	£ s. d.	£ s. d.	£ s. d.
Clare,	264	6,136 9 0	8,610 8 10	4,850 11 10	2,498 11 0
Cork,	651	22,851 9 10	34,372 4 11	19,347 5 11	3,595 13 4
Galway,	4,537	23,541 7 0	27,080 11 5	20,710 8 5	2,745 0 5
Kerry,	536	22,946 13 3	23,871 13 0	31,618 0 4	16,765 19 5
Leitrim,	5	100 0 0	105 10 10	105 10 10	3,115 13 8
Limerick,	8	662 10 0	631 8 8	614 18 5	3,451 5 8
Mayo,	1,477	14,923 14 0	18,625 16 11	13,661 16 11	2,348 13 5
Sligo,	367	5,472 8 0	5,733 17 0	1,965 0 11	3,075 1 11
Roscommon,	1	1,600 0 0	1,643 18 1	655 13 1	8,785 0 10
Tipperary,	1	1,700 0 0	1,767 4 7	195 4 7	3,543 10 9
Total,	5,600	100,481 4 1	104,574 5 0	85,363 9 11	46,115 11 0

The above totals include 430 loans for £6,332 made in the year, as compared with 556 loans for £7,084 in the previous year. The repayments in the year amounted to £6,308 as compared with £7,383 in 1889. The arrears of instalments recoverable amount to £1,876, compared with £2,637 in the previous year.

SEA AND COAST FISHERIES FUND.

The following statement shows the total amount advanced on loan for fishery purposes in each of the maritime counties to 31st December, 1890, the date of the last Parliamentary Return, and the total repayments to same date :—

County.	No. of Loans	Total Amount advanced to 31st December, 1890.	Total Amount to be repaid, including interest at the rate of 2½ per cent. per annum.	Repayments to 31st December, 1890.	Balance available for Loan, being Cash Balances and Consols in credit on 1st January, 1891.
		£ s. d.	£ s. d.	£ s. d.	£ s. d.
General.—Loans made by late Trustees,	696	15,780 0 0	17,438 19 9	15,632 4 9	23,776 17 3
Antrim,	13	233 15 5	233 14 0	191 4 5	
Cork,	43	7,201 0 0	8,618 10 1	6,845 17 11	
Donegal,	976	3,233 14 10	4,169 4 5	3,982 19 4	
Down,	35	3,373 10 0	3,658 15 1	1,415 11 0	
Dublin,	31	8,856 10 0	10,851 5 6	5,535 8 9	
Galway,	192	3,609 0 0	3,544 8 9	3,593 15 6	
Londonderry,	16	231 0 0	287 13 5	180 13 9	
Louth,	9	535 0 0	710 16 6	135 5 9	
Mayo,	104	784 5 0	877 3 9	770 8 8	
Meath,	1	10 0 0	10 10 0	10 10 0	
Waterford,	30	1,254 0 0	1,377 15 10	837 11 3	
Wexford,	34	843 0 0	363 1 5	353 11 10	
Wicklow,	77	5,334 0 0	5,594 8 9	5,188 13 6	
Total,	1,333	54,839 15 1	54,404 15 3	39,049 3 10	

advanced during the year, as compared with 81 loans for £4,777 in 1889, and the repayments for the same period amounted to £5,133, as compared with £5,998 for 1889. The arrears stand at £2,785, of which £1,348 is irrecoverable, as compared with £2,318 in the previous year, the greater portion of which are in respect of loans made by the late Trustees.

NATIONAL MONUMENTS AND ECCLESIASTICAL RUINS.

(Irish Church Act, 1869.)

32 and 33 Vic., cap. 42, s. 25.

All works necessary for the maintenance of the several structures vested in the Board for preservation as National Monuments have been attended to.

POST ROADS.

Act 6 & 7 Wm. IV., cap. 116, section 61.

The repairs were effected to the following post roads :—

Co. TIPPERARY.—Tipperary to Limerick Junction.
Co. CORK.—Courtmacsherry to Timoleague.

COUNTY SURVEYORS' ASSISTANTS.

Nine candidates for the office of County Surveyors' Assistants have been examined under the warrant of the Lord Lieutenant, pursuant to the provisions of the Act 6 & 7 Wm. IV., c. 116, and their qualifications certified to the County Surveyors.

LIMITED OWNERS' RESIDENCES (SETTLED ESTATES ACTS).

An application has been received under these Acts, but no Order has been made; the matter is proceeding. The Order has been made in the case of the application which was stated to be under consideration in last year's Report.

ARBITRATIONS, UNDER "THE RAILWAYS (IRELAND) ACTS,"

(1851, 1860, 1864),

14 & 15 Vic., c. 70 23 & 24 Vic., c. 97; and 27 & 28 Vic., c. 71.

Arbitrations have been applied for and Arbitrators appointed for the following, viz :—

Railway Companies :

The Ballinrobe and Claremorris Light Railway Company.
The Kingstown and Kingsbridge Junction Railway Company.
The South Clare Railway Company.
The Bray and Enniskerry Railway Company.
The Midland Great Western of Ireland Railway Company.
The Great Southern and Western of Ireland Railway Company (2).

Commissioners :

The Belfast City and District Water Commissioners.

Boards of Guardians of Poor Law Unions :

Dundalk, Killadysert, Kilmallock, Mullingar, Longford, Ballycastle, Kells, Roscrea, Millstreet, Edenderry, Listowel, Macroom, Carrickmacross, Ennis, Navan, Mountmellick—For purposes of Labourers (Ireland) Acts, 46 & 47 Vic., c. 60, and 48 & 49 Vic., c. 77.

Lismore—Cappoquin Waterworks.

Glin—Foynes Waterworks.

Tralee—Castleisland Waterworks.

RECEIVER ACCOUNTS FOR LOANS.

We continue to be in possession of the Southern and the Letterkenny Railways. The gross earnings of the Southern Railway in the year 1890 amounted to £9,929, and after paying for haulage, rent to the Great Southern, and other charges, there remained a surplus of £2,189. We received from the County Tipperary and the individual guarantors the sum of £3,145, to pay the dividend at the rate of 5 per cent. per annum on the guaranteed stock, amounting to £62,900, which has been duly paid over to the shareholders holding that Stock.

The gross receipts of the Letterkenny Railway in the year 1890 amounted to £6,393, as compared with £5,855 in 1889, the surplus revenue being £1,719.

Our Receiver over the Galway Harbour Revenues reports a gross receipt in the year to 31st March last of £3,878 9s. 5d. We paid over to the National Debt Commissioners in the same time £3,190 8s., the balance being required for the maintenance of the harbour.

IV.—LIGHT RAILWAYS.

TRAMWAYS AND LIGHT RAILWAYS UNDER THE ACT OF 1883.

TRAMWAYS ACTS, 23 & 24 Vic., c. 152 (1860); 24 & 25 Vic., c. 102 (1861); 34 & 35 Vic., c. 114 (1871); 44 & 45 Vic., c. 17 (1881); and 46 & 47 Vic., c. 43 (1883).

Under the provisions of the Tramways Acts of 1860 and 1861 we are required, on the application of the promoters of tramway and light railway projects, to cause an inquiry to be held into the merits of the undertakings from an engineering point of view, and to any modification in that respect which may be advantageously made, and to report our opinion thereon. These reports are directed to be submitted to the Grand Juries for their consideration in approving of the proposals made, prior to granting a baronial guarantee on the amount of capital required for the carrying out of any proposed undertaking, and to an Order of the Lord Lieutenant in Council being sought.

The cost of these inquiries has been defrayed out of funds deposited in our hands by the Promoters.

The following cases were brought forward for inquiry at last Summer and Spring Assizes, and were duly reported on by the Board :—Donoughmore Extension; Tuam and Claremorris; Kilfala and Ballycastle; Clonakilty and Rosscarbery; Tuam and Ballyhaunis; Loughrea and Woodford; Swinford and Foxford; Ballina and Crossmolina, of which the four first named received the requisite guarantee on their capital.

Our duty in connexion with guaranteed undertakings is that prescribed by the 10th section, subsection 4, of the Tramways Act of 1883, which enacts that before any Order in Council is made authorising the carrying out of a guaranteed project, we are required to furnish the Lord Lieutenant in Council with an estimate of the amount of paid-up capital which will be necessary for the purposes of the undertaking. The estimates having been examined and checked for that purpose, are submitted to the Privy Council at the hearing of applications for Orders authorizing the construction of any line of tramway or light railway, and the Engineers who checked these estimates attend at the hearing and are examined thereon. The following table shows the applications which have been passed by the Privy Council under this Act, together with the valuation of guaranteeing areas, &c., &c. :—

The total mileage of projects guaranteed is 398 miles, viz. (see Nos. I. and II. in following list), and the guaranteed capital £1,256,112. The Orders have lapsed in five other cases, amounting to £191,200, detailed at III.

GUARANTEED UNDERTAKINGS passed by PRIVY COUNCIL.

I.—CONSTRUCTED AND OPENED TO THE PUBLIC.

Name of Project.	No. of Miles.	Promoters' Guarantee.	Board's Guarantee.	Amount of Guarantee.	Guaranteeing Area. County.	Baronies.	Valuation.
Castlederg Railway Light Railway.	1				Antrim.	Co. of Town of Castlederg.	
Cavan, Leitrim, and Roscommon Light Railway.	48				Cavan. Leitrim.		
West Clare Light Railway.	27				Clare.		
Ballymoney and Tisraigan Light Railway.	8				Cork.		
Cork, Cornkduid, and Slattery Light Railway.	16						
Schull and Skibbereen Light Railway.	14						
Dublin and Blessington Steam Tramway.	13				Dublin and Wicklow.		
Cloghan Valley Tramway.	24						
West Donegal Light Railway	4				Donegal.		
Muckishmore and Fintown Light Railway.	19				Cork.		
Tralee and Dingle Light Railway.	37				Kerry.		
Timoleague and Courtmacsherry.	8				Cork.		

II.—LINES IN PROGRESS OF CONSTRUCTION.

Name of Project.	No. of Miles.				County.	Baronies.	Valuation.
Loughrea and Attymon Light Railway.	9				Galway.		
Ballinrobe and Claremorris Light Railway.	13				Mayo.		
South Clare Light Railway.	26				Clare.		
Tuam and Claremorris.	17				Mayo.		

Total I. and II.

III.—LINES WHERE THE ORDERS HAVE EXPIRED.

An amount is provided in the Estimates to enable us to meet any contributions which may become payable in respect of the two per cent. guaranteed by Government under the 8th Section of the "Tramways (Ireland) Act, 1883."

We have paid in the year, in respect of the two per cent. guaranteed by the Treasury under this section of the Act of 1883, a sum of £12,109, reducing the amount contributed by counties for dividend purposes from £29,925 to £17,816, in addition to which a sum of £2,490 was levied on the Baronies to defray the excess of expenditure over receipts on some of the lines. A General Statistical Return is appended (vide Appendix D), showing the incidence of taxation, &c., &c., on the several areas charged under guarantees, and Map attached shows the Lines under the Acts of 1883 and 1889.

LIGHT RAILWAYS (IRELAND) ACT, 1889,

52 and 53 Vic., c. 66 ;

RAILWAYS (IRELAND) ACT, 1890,

53 and 54 Vic., c. 52 ;

TRANSFER OF RAILWAYS (IRELAND) ACT, 1890,

54 Vic., c. 2.

The several schemes recommended by the Board in their Statutory Reports were brought before the Grand Juries at the Spring Assizes of 1890, and the tabulated statement appended sets forth the financial bearings, &c., of these recommendations and shows the action taken thereon by the Grand Juries. The projects were guaranteed and approved, subject to certain modifications in the Statutory Reports, with the exception of two, viz., the line from Buncrana to Carndonagh, which was guaranteed, but the Judge refused to fiat the presentment owing to the promoters not having signified in their advertisement notice their intention of applying for a guarantee ; and the line from Letterkenny to Crossroads, in which the Grand Jury disapproved of the particular route.

County.	Lines.	M.		Expends.	Free Grant.	Guarantee.	Action of Grand Juries.
				£	£	£	
Donegal, -	Donegal and Killybegs, ,	18¾	N.	116,000	115,800	1,000	Guaranteed.
" -	Stranorlar and Glenties, ,	24¼	N.	116,000	115,000	1,000	Do.
" -	Letterkenny and Crossroads, ,	42	N.	126,000	125,000	1,000	Disapproved.
" -	Buncrana and Carndonagh, ,	18¼	N.	67,500	52,500	15,000	Guaranteed, but presentment not fiated.
Mayo, -	Ballina and Belmullet, ,	38¼	N.	154,000	153,000	1,000	Guaranteed.
" -	Westport and Mallaranny, ,	18	B.	110,100	109,100	1,000	Do.
" -	Ballina and Ballysodare, ,	18	B.	74,500	73,500	1,000	Do.
Galway, -	Galway and Clifden, ,	49½	B.	345,500	344,500	1,000	Do.
Kerry, -	Headford and Kenmare, ,	18¼	B.	110,000	50,000	60,000	Do.
" -	Killorglin and Valencia, ,	26¼	B.	156,000	85,000	70,000	Do.
Cork, -	Baltimore Extension, ,	7¾	B.	45,700	45,700	—	Approved.
" -	Bantry Bay Extension, ,	1½	B.	20,800	20,800	—	Do.
Down, ,	Downpatrick and Ardglass, ,	8	B.	51,000	30,000	17,000	Guaranteed.

Pursuant to the condition as regarded funds appended to the several notifications in the *Dublin Gazette* scheduling the lines, your Lordships reserved the decision as to which lines were to be aided having regard to the funds available under the Act.

For the purpose of convening Grand Juries at Special Sessions in order to remedy informalities in certain of the presentments, and to enable existing Railway Companies to construct, maintain, and work railways other than Light Railways, the Railways (Ireland) Act, 1890, received legislative sanction on the 18th August, 1890.

As a result of protracted negociations, mainly under the immediate direction of the Financial Secretary to the Treasury, with the promoters and the Railway Companies, the following scheme was eventually formulated with your Lordships' approval, and Orders in Council were duly obtained, with the exception of the case of Strancorlar and Glenties, in regard to which matters are still pending :—

County.	Line.	Miles.	Gauge.	Working Railway Company.	First Grant.	Guarantee.	Date of Order in Council.
					£	£	
Donegal,	Donegal and Killybegs,	19	N.	West Donegal,	118,600	1,000	24th Oct., 1890.
Do.,	Strancorlar and Glenties,	31½	N.	Finn Valley,	115,000	1,000	Not executed.
Mayo,	Westport and Mallaranny,	18	B.	Midland Great Western,	131,400	—	1st Dec., 1890.
Do.,	Ballina and Killala,	8	B.	do.,	44,000	—	1st Dec., 1890.
Galway,	Galway and Clifden,	48	B.	do.,	264,600	—	1st Dec., 1890.
Kerry,	Headford and Kenmare,	19½	B.	Great Southern and Western,	50,000	40,000	17th Feb., 1891.
Do.,	Killorglin and Valentia,	22½	B.	do.,	65,000	70,000	17th Feb., 1891.
Cork,	Baltimore Extension,	7½	B.	Cork, Bandon, and South Coast Company,	55,700	—	17th Feb., 1891.
Do.,	Bantry Bay Extension,	1½	B.	do.,	15,000	—	20th Jan., 1891
Down,	Downpatrick and Ardglass	8	B.	Belfast and Co. Down Company.	30,000	—	29th Nov., 1890.
				Total,	905,900	138,000	

ordinary circumstances have been possible. The extent of the employment afforded to the end of the financial year will be seen from the table below :—

Railway.	Maximum Number of Men Employed for Week ending											
	Jan. 1.	Feb. 1.	Mar. 1.	Apr. 1.	May 1.	June 1.	July 1.	Aug. 1.	Sep. 1.	Oct. 1.	Nov. 1.	Dec. 1.
Donegal and Killybegs,												
Galway and Clifden,												
Westport and Mallaranny,												
Ballinrobe and Achill,												
Galway and Clifden,												
Killorglin and Valentia,												
Headford and Kenmare,												
Gweedore and Ballina,												
Bantry Extension,												
Crossmolina and Achill,												
Collooney and Claremorris,												
Parsonstown and Glanties,												
Total—Maximum,												
Do. Minimum,												
Weekly average,												

The Transfer of Railways (Ireland) Act, 1890, which received the Royal Assent on 9th December, whilst giving powers to promoters to agree for transfer of their undertakings to existing Railway Companies, contained a provision (s. 17) enabling promoters to enter on lands in anticipation of Arbitrators' awards, while preserving the rights of owners and occupiers, and the power given by that section was promptly availed of.

This anticipatory action, by which no less than 312 miles of railway were commenced in advance of the usual contract plans, &c., necessarily threw an immense amount of work on this department, greatly straining its resources; but so far the results in giving an amount of employment which could not otherwise have been so usefully afforded, have been satisfactory and cordially recognised by Government. It is also right to observe that the several Railway Companies and their Officials and the Contractors co-operated most heartily, often at much personal inconvenience.

On the 30th December, 1890, the lines Mallaranny and Achill Sound, Collooney and Swinford, Swinford and Claremorris, were scheduled under the 2nd section of the Light Railways Act of 1889, and two sets of promoters came forward for the lines from Collooney and Claremorris, viz., the Collooney and Claremorris Junction Light Railways and Tramways Company, Limited, and the Athenry and Tuam Railway Company, Limited, made lodgments in pursuance of the 2nd section of the Tramways Act of 1860, on the 15th January last, and the inquiry prescribed by the 9th section of that Act was held before the Board's Investigators, Major-General C. S. Hutchinson, R.E., C.B., John G. Barton, C.E., M.I.C.E., and Edwin Liller, at Claremorris, Swinford, and Collooney on the 25th, 27th, and 29th idem. We issued our Statutory Report on the 28th February, with your Lordships' approval, and the varying conditions of the grants in aid and guarantees are given below.

The Grand Jury of Sligo, at Spring Assizes, made a presentment guaranteeing 4 per cent. on £80,000 in favour of the company first above-named, who propose to work the line from Collooney to Swinford through the Sligo, Leitrim, and Northern Counties Railway Company, and they passed a resolution signifying that if the line were made through to Claremorris they would be prepared to guarantee £10,000 additional.

The Grand Jury of Mayo at Spring Assizes presented for 4 per cent. on £40,000 for the line from Swinford to Claremorris in favour of the Athenry and Tuam Railway Company.

Both proposed working companies are, it is said, in accord as to the system of through working.

Lodgments were also made on 15th January, 1891, in the case of two rival schemes in Donegal connecting the district of Letterkenny with that of Gweedore, viz., the Letterkenny and Gweedore Light Railway, the Letterkenny and Dunfanaghy Coast Light Railway, and the inquiries were held at Letterkenny on 6th and 7th February, at Bunbeg on 10th February, and at Dunfanaghy on 11th February, before our Investigators, Major Handley Kirkwood, R.E., Mr. R. F. Fleming, C.E., M.I.C.E., and S. B. Humphreys.

The Board issued their Statutory Report with your Lordships' sanction, under date the 11th March, in favour of the former project (40 miles long), declaring the capital necessary at £357,500. The Grand Jury made a presentment at the Spring Assizes fixing the baronial guarantee of 5 per cent. on £1,000 for working and maintaining the line to the first six years from the date of the opening of the undertaking, but owing to this last condition, the presentment could not be accepted.

We have the honour to be

Your Lordships' obedient Servants,

R. H. SANKEY,
W. R. LE FANU,
S. U. ROBERTS,
H. O'SHAUGHNESSY,

Commissioners
of
Public Works
in Ireland.

W. R. Boary, Secretary.

Office of Public Works, Dublin,

18th July, 1891.

APPENDICES.

APPENDIX A.—

(A.)—Abstract of the Accounts of the Commissioners of Public Works in Ireland, shewing the Total of

	Page	Heads of Account.	Reference to Blue Book, 189.	Ireland.
			£ s. d.	£ s. d.
A 1	38	Parliamentary Votes and Grants, viz.—		
		1. Public Works and Buildings, Ireland.		
		2. Public Works Office, Ireland.		
		3. Exchequer—Extra Receipts.	30,412 16 1	446,877 16 6
A 2	44	Loans Advanced,	8,900 10 1	908,920 0 0
A 3	46	Loans Repayments,	—	921,920 6 2
A 4	48	Land Improvement Proklamation. 20 Vic., c. 32,	841 0 0	1,797 0 0
A 5	50	District Lunatic Asylums,	4,025 10 1	28,000 2 0
A 6	66	Sea Fisheries, Ireland, 16 & 17 Vic., c. 84,	1,000 6 6	7,925 16 1
A 7	58	Miscellaneous Services, viz.—		
		1. Deposit Accounts, 1 & 2 Wm. IV., c. 33, &c.		
		2. Railway and other Arbitrations, 14 & 15 Vic., c. 70.		
		3. Arterial Drainage Deposits, 26 & 27 Vic., c. 88, &c.		
		4. Piers—Maintenance, 15 & 17 Vic., c. 138.		
		5. Inland Navigation—Shannon.		
		6. Drainage Maintenance, 29 & 30 Vic., c. 49.		
		7. National Monuments, 32 & 33 Vic., c. 42.	14,346 10 10	74,894 10 0
		8. Liffey Hall.		
		9. Irish Reproductive Loan Fund, 47 & 48 Vic., c. 68,		
		10. Sea and Coast Fisheries Loan Fund,		
		11. Galway Harbour Receiver's Account,		
		12. Southern Railway,		
		13. Letterkenny Railway,		
		14. Emigration Grants,		
		15. Sundry Accounts,		
		Total.	45,472 15 0	2,152,651 9 1
A 8	66	Statement of Final Awards under Arterial Drainage Act, 26 & 27 Vic., c. 88, with Repayments thereon, to the 31st March, 1891.		

ACCOUNTS.

Sums Intrusted to their Management for Collection or Disbursement for Year ended 31st March, 1891.

Amount produces the Funds etc.	Coupon	Commission Discount Case Accounts Guar Rent Board etc.	Paid	Charges on Cost Works etc.	Remit
£ s. d.	£ s. d.	£ s. d.	£ s. d.	£ s. d.	£ s. d.
—	679,368 13 6	—	632,195 18 9	37,114 15 4	679,368 11 6
—	794,440 10 3	—	804,606 16 10	81,654 18 6	794,660 18 8
—	121,360 6 3	—	121,360 3 9	—	121,676 4 2
—	3,000 11 8	—	1,901 7 11	457 9 4	3,000 11 8
—	14,100 18 6	—	82,853 2 3	8,106 11 9	14,100 16 4
—	3,000 1 4	—	6,003 17 2	3,000 4 4	3,000 1 4
—	82,345 10 10	—	64,630 17 10	14,434 18 9	84,345 10 10
—	8,965,174 13 1	—	2,157,201 6 30	163,743 9 3	3,965,174 13 1

An Account showing the Receipts and Expenditure of the Commissioners

(A 1.)—PARLIAMENTARY

RECEIPTS.	£ s. d.	£ s. d.	£ s. d.
Balance from last Account, ...	—	—	30,418 15 1
I. PUBLIC BUILDINGS.			
Vote for the year 1890-91, ...	373,573 0 0		
Supplementary Vote, . . .	128,500 0 0	400,073 0 0	
Purchase of Sites and Buildings, . .	—	—	
NEW WORKS AND ALTERATIONS :—			
Transfers and Readjustments, .	—	396 3 6	
Carried forward, .	—	400,871 3 6	30,418 15 1

of Public Works in the Year ended 31st March, 1891.

VOTES AND GRANTS.

EXPENDITURE.	£ s. d.	£ s. d.	£ s. d.
Balances on Parliamentary Vote surrendered to H.M. Exchequer, viz.:—			
Public Buildings, .	—	15,406 5 5	
Office of Public Works, :	—	1,583 19 1	16,989 14 4
1. Public Buildings.			
Purchase of Sites and Buildings, . .	—	500 0 0	
New Works and Alterations:—			
Royal Hospital, .	3,906 15 1		
Constabulary Buildings, .	7,681 5 8		
Naval Reserve Buildings, .	47 5 5		
Ordnance Survey Office, .	819 5 11		
Chief Secretary's Office—Veterinary Department, .	63 5 4		
Kingstown Police Court, .	547 19 11		
Constabulary Buildings, .	11,617 8 0		
Dundrum Criminal Lunatic Asylum, .	118 17 10		
Science and Art Buildings, .	9,355 14 8		
Botanic Gardens, Glasnevin, .	831 4 0		
Bankruptcy Court, .	419 7 7		
Probate Office, .	3 7 8		
National Education Buildings:—	£ s. d.		
Metropolitan Buildings—Workshops,	255 14 6		
Ordinary Literary Schools, .	37,331 8 0		
Teachers' Residences,	64 16 0	37,650 17 6	
Queen's College, Belfast, .	45 16 11		
Inland Revenue Office, Galway, .	357 3 1		
Postal and Telegraph Buildings, .	1,517 8 0		
Phoenix Park, .	869 11 5		
Kingstown Harbour—Mail Packet Pier, .	3,357 0 0		
Royal University, .	434 0 9		
Clare Slob Reclamation, .	1,159 4 4	69,711 3 0	
Carried forward, .	—	70,211 3 0	16,989 14 4

An Account showing the Receipts and Expenditure of the Commissioners

(A 1.)—PARLIAMENTARY

RECEIPTS—continued.

	£ s. d.	£ s. d.	£ s. d.
Brought forward,		409,671 3 6	20,619 18 1
1. PUBLIC BUILDINGS—continued.			
TRANSFERS AND REIMBURSEMENTS:—			
Maintenance and Supplies,	740 16 10		
Furniture, Fittings, &c.,	24 19 2		
Rents,	1 0 0		
Fuel, Light, Water, &c.,	538 9 11		
Drainage Works—River Shannon,	109 13 1		
		1,414 9 0	411,085 12 6

of Public Works in the Year ended 31st March, 1891—*continued.*

VOTES AND GRANTS—*continued.*

EXPENDITURE—*continued.*

				Post, Light-house, Cleaning, &c.	Lands				
	£ s. d.	£ s. d.	£ s. d.	£ s. d.	£ s. d.	£ s. d.	£ s. d.
Brought forward .	—	—	—	—	—	70,941 6 0	16,689 10 0
PUBLIC BUILDINGS—con.							
...							
Total . . .	7,644 5 7	13,659 14 1	10,800 7 11	10,123 13	3,310,21 3 4	129,881 0 4	
					Carried forward, . .	100,673 5 6	16,640 15 6

An Account showing the Receipts and Expenditure of the Commissioners

(A 1.)—PARLIAMENTARY

RECEIPTS—continued.	£ s. d.	£ s. d.	£ s. d.
Brought forward,	—	—	431,498 7 7
Public Buildings—continued.			
Contributions in Aid of Building National Schools :—	—	—	84 0 0
2. Offices of Public Works (Class II.) :—			
Vote,	—	37,661 0 0	
Transfers and Refunds,	—	131 5 9	37,792 5 9
3. Engineers Extra Receipts :—			
Public Buildings :—			
Rents,	3,847 1 6		
Sales, &c., including £100 for Land at Leek Prices,	616 3 3	4,463 4 7	
Royal Parks :—			
Rents for Grazing, &c.,	11 8 0		
Sales,	193 10 1	204 18 1	
Kingstown Harbour :—			
Dues,	1,318 4 7		
Rents,	384 6 2		
Water supplied to Shipping,	133 16 0		
Ballast,	101 18 7		
Fire of Planks and Graves,	84 10 0		
Rent Licenses,	6 13 0		
Sale of Land at Dalkey,	88 8 8	1,989 16 4	
Howth Harbour :—			
Dues,	83 14 6		
Rents,	249 6 2	335 0 8	
Dunglandee Harbour :—			
Rents,	—	15 1 0	
Ardglass Harbour :—			
Rents,	4 15 0		
Dues,	154 7 8		
Sales,	16 13 8	175 15 11	
Donaghadee Harbour :—			
Rents,	59 11 1		
Dues,	28 10 7	79 4 8	
Maigue Navigation :—			
Tolls,	—	7 11 1	
Boyne Navigation :—			
Rent,	0 10 0		
Tolls,	163 8 3	163 18 3	
			7,344 0 7

of Public Works in the Year ended 31st March, 1891.

VOTES AND GRANTS—continued.

EXPENDITURE—continued.	£ s. d.	£ s. d.	£ s. d.
Brought forward, . .	—	103,079 6 4	19,408 16 6
1. Public Buildings—continued.			
Repayments to Baronies, Tramways and Public Companies (Ireland) Act, 1883,	—	22,109 0 4	
Light Railways (Ireland) Act, 1889, 52 & 53 Vic., c. 66,	—	116,408 16 9	
Special Railway Works,	—	30,120 13 9	
Drainage Works—River Shannon,	—	3,657 17 11	136,067 0 6
Contribution in Aid of Building National Schools,	—	—	90 0 0
2. Office of Public Works (Class II.) :—			
Salaries,	—	25,647 11 8	
Travelling Expenses,	—	5,673 4 4	
Incidental Expenses,	—	198 10 10	
Land Improvement and Land Law Act, Salaries, and Expenses,	—	3,633 1 10	34,004 4 3
3. Surveyors, Extra Receipts :—			
Public Buildings :— Sums refunded,	9 10 0		
Howth Harbour :— Taxes refunded,	8 13 2		
Kingstown Harbour :— Ballast,	44 10 6		
Phœnix Park :— Refund of over-charge for Grazing,	33 5 0	53 7 6	
Office of Public Works :— Deposits refunded, Land Law Act, sec. 22 ; and Townlands,	—	67 6 0	
Transferred to H. M. Exchequer,	—	10,376 13 4	10,376 13 0
			612,120 10 2
Balance,	—	—	37,114 19 4
			479,840 13 6

F. L. Wrenn, Accountant.

(A 2.)—An Account showing the Receipts and Expenditure of the Commissioners

PUBLIC WORKS LOAN

	£ s. d.	£ s. d.
To Balance, 31st March, 1890,	—	9,560 18 8
„ Public Works Loans:—		
Vote of Credit 1889-90, £1,000,000—National Debt Commissioners,	170,000 0 0	
„ 1890-91, £3,000,000— „	525,000 0 0	
		695,000 0 0
		704,560 18 2

of Public Works in the Year ended 31st March, 1891.

ADVANCES.

	£ s. d.	£ s. d.
By Public Works Loans,		
Amount advanced on Loans, viz.:—		
Grand Juries of Counties,	8,853 0 0	
Local Boards,	1,000 0 0	
Inland Navigation,	16,000 0 0	
Public Buildings,	3,080 0 0	
Railways,	—	
Harbours, Docks, &c.,	8,500 0 0	
Raising of the Working Classes,	80,070 0 0	
Glebe Loan, 33 & 34 Vic., c. 112,	30,618 4 6	
Public Health, 37 & 38 Vic., c. 93,	70,308 1 7	
Drainage Maintenance, 39 & 40 Vic., c. 49, &c.,	450 0 0	
District Drainage Bonds, 26 & 27 Vic., c. 88,	14,188 0 0	
Fiat Bonds, for Repairs, 4 & 7 Wm. IV., c. 116,	108 3 4	
Land Improvement Preliminary Expenses,	1,080 0 0	
Repairs of Fishery Piers,	999 4 11	
Lunatic Asylums Buildings, 1 & 2 Geo. IV., c. 85,	30,048 3 11	
Labourers' Acts,	138,185 0 0	
Land Improvement, 10 Vic., c. 32, &c.,	59,736 0 0	
National School Teachers' Residences,	13,168 0 0	
Dispensary Houses,	8,900 10 0	
New-Vested Schools and Training Colleges,	8,041 0 0	
Land Law, 44 & 45 Vic., c. 49, c. 31,	46,040 0 0	
Seed Supply Act, 1880,	343,908 6 8	684,026 16 10
Balance unissued,	—	20,524 19 4
		704,550 16 2

(A 3.)—An Account showing the Receipts and Expenditure of the Commissioners
PUBLIC WORKS LOANS

	Repayments	Total
	£ s. d.	£ s. d.
To Public Works Loans:—		
Amounts received in repayment:—		
Grand Juries of Counties,	8,201 12 5	
Local Boards,	62,742 4 1	
Roads and Bridges,	10,042 1 2	
Inland Navigations,	3,524 3 4	
Public Buildings,	1,280 10 3	
Railways,	71,784 5 1	
Quarries, Mines and Miscellaneous,	63 16 3	
Harbours, Docks, &c.,	30,806 15 5	
Fishery Piers and Harbours,	118 9 7	
Labourers' Dwellings in Towns,	12,601 11 1	
Artisans' Dwellings,	31,478 19 0	
Housing of the Working Classes,	31,828 4 9	
Glebe Loans,	21,935 15 6	
Public Health,	328,043 9 5	
River Drainage and Navigation, 5 & 6 Vic., c. 89,	143 16 2	
River Drainage Maintenance, 10 & 50 Vic., c. 49, &c.,	2,950 2 10	
River Drainage, 24 & 27 Vic., c. 99,	26,573 10 10	
Loans per Act 27 Geo. III., c. 84,	180 0 0	
Foot Roads, Repairs,	290 3 1	
Land Improvement Preliminary Expenses,	60d 12 9	
Repairs of Fishery Piers,	29 1 5	
Lunatic Asylums Buildings,	29,477 8 1	
Building Schools,	76 11 0	
Relief of Distress,	197 5 0	
Seed Supply, 1880,	2,651 7 3	
Seed Supply, 1890,	1,224 1 11	
Emigration,	638 9 9	
Labourers' Acts,	32,204 3 6	
Land Improvement Loans,	104,544 9 10	
National School Teachers' Residences,	6,175 11 0	
Dispensary Houses,	2,201 0 8	
Reformed Schools and Training Colleges,	1,142 2 6	
Land Law, 44 & 45 Vic., c. 49, c. 61,	42,540 1 3	
Land Act Loans, 33 & 34 Vic., c. 46,	19,428 3 10	
		570,007 18 6
Church Fund Loans:—		
Land Improvement,	91,457 6 0	
Sanitary,	1,534 4 7	
Baronial Works,	17,599 14 9	
Relief of Distress,	870 5 10	
Arterial Drainage,	99 0 8	
		61,590 11 5
		931,598 5 5

Office of Public Works, Dublin, 1st May, 1891.

(A 4.)—LAND IMPROVEMENT

RECEIPTS.	£ s. d.	£ s. d.
Balance from last Account,	—	241 4 6
Amount received from National Debt Commissioners by way of Loan,	1,000 0 0	
" " from Proprietors in Repayment of Preliminary Expenses,	797 8 9	1,797 8 9
		2,038 11 3

Office of Public Works, Dublin, 1st May, 1891.

of Public Works, in the Year ended 31st March, 1891.

DEPARTMENTS.

		£ s. d.	£ s. d.
By transfer to National Debt Commissioners,	.	—	870,027 15 6
By transfer to Irish Land Commissioners,	.	—	51,900 11 6
			911,928 5 8

F. L. Wrenn, Accountant.

(A 5.)—LUNATIC

An Account showing the Receipts and Expenditure by the Commissioners of Public Works, Ireland, for 1891, pursuant to Act 1 & 2

RECEIPTS.	£ s. d.	£ s. d.	£ s. d.
Balance from last Account,	—	—	4,025 13 1
Amounts received from the Public Works Loan Fund on account of Loans to the following District Asylums :—			
Armagh,	—	800 0 0	
Ballinasloe,	—	3,500 0 0	
Castlebar,	—	6,000 0 0	
Clonmel,	704 12 1	742 11 10	
Sale of old materials,	35 10 9		
Cork,	—	7,800 0 0	
Enniscorthy,	—	317 14 1	
Killarney,	—	3,450 0 0	
Limerick,	—	171 13 8	
Londonderry,	—	2,500 0 0	
Monaghan,	—	3,500 0 0	
Mullingar,	—	3,000 0 0	
Omagh,	—	1,000 0 0	
Richmond,	—	800 0 0	
Waterford,	—	800 0 0	30,083 5 5
			34,108 16 9

Office of Public Works, Dublin, 1st May, 1891.

(A 6.)—SEA FISHERIES

An Account showing the Receipts and Expenditure by the Commissioners of Public Works,

RECEIPTS.	£ s. d.	£ s. d.	£ s. d.
Balance from last Account,	—	—	1,038 6 1
Amount received from the Land Law Commissioners on account of Grant of £150,000,	—	6,000 0 0	
Amounts received as Contribution—			
Ballycotton Harbour,	—	160 0 0	
Amounts received in repayment of Loans—			
Ballymoney Pier,	33 16 6		
Ballyhack Pier,	43 1 4		
Lenamore Harbour,	211 2 5		
Kilkee Ron: Slip,	36 13 6		
Annalong Harbour,	73 16 6		
Kilkeel Harbour,	158 16 6		
Cahill Pier,	12 13 7		
Port Salon Pier,	30 19 4		
Portstewart Harbour,	74 10 0		
Malin Head Pier,	111 10 10		
Clogga Pier,	319 11 10		
Carlingford Harbour,	224 13 10		
Carrigaholt Harbour,	148 3 5		
Kilmore Harbour,	314 6 3	1,773 15 1	7,933 14 1
			8,963 1 8

Office of Public Works, Dublin, 1st May, 1891.

ASYLUMS BUILDINGS.

Account of the Commissioners for the Control, &c., of Lunatic Asylums) during the year ended 31st March, Geo. IV., c. 33, &c, &c.

EXPENDITURE			£ s. d.	£ s. d.	£ s. d.
Amounts expended on the following District Asylums, viz:—					
Armagh,	.	.	—	500 0 0	
Ballinasloe,	.	.	—	2,315 0 7	
Castlebar,	.	.	—	4,010 14 3	
Clonmel,	.	.	—	685 6 7	
Cork, .	.	.	—	6,640 0 10	
Enniscorthy,	.	.	—	356 1 8	
Kilkenny,	.	.	—	4,705 14 0	
Limerick,	.	.	—	209 4 6	
Londonderry,	.	.	—	3,461 1 6	
Maryboro,	.	.	—	5,660 6 7	
Mullingar,	.	.	—	3,268 11 11	
Omagh,	.	.	—	778 1 10	
Richmond,	.	.	—	733 13 6	
Waterford,	.	.	—	735 7 8	33,000 2 9
Balance,	.	.	—	—	1,105 11 0
					34,105 18 9

F. L. WORK, Accountant.

(IRELAND) COMMISSION.

IRELAND, during the Year ended 31st March, 1891, pursuant to Act 46 & 47 Victoria, cap. 38.

EXPENDITURE			£ s. d.	£ s. d.	£ s. d.
Expenses of Engineering Staff, .	.	.	—	883 13 10	
Amounts expended on the following Works:—					
Knocknadoog Pier,	.	.	50 16 1		
Bunfield Pier,	.	.	9 5 0		
Passage East Harbour,	.	.	3,175 0 4		
Ballyvoyle Harbour,	.	.	600 1 3		
Clogher Head Breakwater,	.	.	1,471 16 10		
Greystones Harbour,	.	.	3,374 14 6	8,770 3 4	6,653 17 2
Balance,	.	.	—	—	2,303 4 3
					8,957 1 5

F. L. WORK, Accountant.

G

(A 7.)—An Account shewing the Receipts and Expenditure by the Commissioners

MISCELLANEOUS

RECEIPTS	£ s. d.	£ s. d.	£ s. d.
To Balance from last Account, ...	—	—	14,344 15 10
1. Deposits for Preliminary Expenses of Loans, &c. :—			
Received from Sundries, ...	—	—	2,385 9 8
2. Railway and other Arbitration Expenses, 14 & 15 Vic., c. 70 :—			
Received from Railway Companies and others, to meet Expenses of Arbitrations, ...	—	—	2,046 13 1
3. Arterial Drainage Deposits, 26 & 27 Vic., c. 88, &c. :—			
Received from Drainage Boards on Account of Preliminary and other Expenses, ...	—	—	148 0 0
4. Piers—Maintenance and Repairs, 16 & 17 Vic., c. 136 :—			
Ballybunion Pier—Transfer from Local Loans Fund, .	—	84 1 1	
Bulganon Pier— Do.,	—	400 0 0	
Claggan Pier— Do.,	—	150 0 0	
Bundoran Pier— Do.,	—	11 3 10	646 4 11
5. Inland Navigation :—			
Shannon River :—			
Rents, . . .	—	2,846 2 8	
Tolls, . .	—	1,287 9 0	
Sales, Refunds, &c.,	—	6 1 3	4,481 14 6
6. Maintenance of Drainage Works, 29 & 30 Vic., c. 49 :—			
Nobber River District, . . .	—	—	414 0 8
7. Shannon Monuments, 32 & 33 Vic., c. 42 :—			
Dividends on Stock, . . .	—	—	637 16 6
Carried forward, . .	—	—	80,867 15 3

of Public Works, Ireland, during the Year ended 31st March, 1891.

SERVICES.

EXPENDITURE	£ s. d.	£ s. d.	£ s. d.
1. Deposits for Preliminary Expenses of Loans, &c. :—			
Paid to Auditors,	—	—	3,975 11 11
2. Railway and other Arbitration Expenses, 14 & 15 Vic., c. 70 :—			
Paid to Valuators, &c.,	—	—	761 19 9
3. Artificial Drainage Deposits, 26 & 27 Vic., c. 88, &c. :—			
Paid for Preliminary Expenses, Arbitrations, &c.,	—	—	47 9 9
4. Piers—Maintenance and Repairs, 16 & 17 Vic., c. 136 :—			
Beantraghee Pier—Labour, Materials, &c.,	—	5 9 0	
Burtonport Pier— Do.,	—	412 14 3	
Clogher Pier— Do.,	—	329 19 1	
Bundoran Pier— Do.,	—	11 9 10	765 13 1
5. Inland Navigation :—			
Shannon River :—			
Maintenance and Repairs of Works,	—	2,804 8 10	
Superintendence, Salaries, and Gratuities,	—	1,194 8 0	
Repayment of Class Canals Pier Loan,	—	484 14 8	
Canal to Trustees of Foynes Harbour on account of the Highway,	—	1,530 0 0	
Law Costs, &c.,	—	98 3 9	4,521 4 9
6. Maintenance of Drainage Works, 29 & 30 Vic., c. 49 :—			
Nobber River District,	—	678 4 4	
Barrigin-Queary District,	—	6 12 0	684 16 4
7. National Monuments, 32 & 33 Vic., c. 43 :—			
Maintenance—			
Salaries and Travelling Expenses of Architects; Caretakers' Wages, Lockkeeps, &c.,	—	633 3 9	
Restoration Works—			
Monasterboice,	10 0 0		
Kilcshee,	119 1 4		
Holy Island, Lough Derg,	165 18 8		
Threakagren,	7 15 0	303 14 0	
Invested in purchase of Stock,	—	1,000 0 0	1,745 17 9
Carried forward,	—	—	14,281 8 8

O 2

(A 7.)—An Account showing the Receipts and Expenditure of the Commissioners

MISCELLANEOUS

RECEIPTS—continued.	£ s. d.	£ s. d.	£ s. d.
Brought forward,	—	—	25,587 19 5
6. Land Hall, 41 Vic., c. 1 :— Rents,	—	—	453 14 4

9. Irish Reproductive Loan Fund, 37 & 38 Vic., c. 86, &c. :—

	Dividends on Stock, &c.	Repayments	
County Clare,	64 17 8	223 0 7	
„ Cork,	89 17 0	1,716 5 4	
„ Galway,	89 5 0	1,564 5 3	
„ Kerry,	380 16 10	469 1 5	
„ Leitrim,	64 16 0	—	
„ Mayo,	81 6 6	1,230 11	
„ Sligo,	46 5 5	345 15 4	
„ Roscommon,	179 18 9	90 10 0	
„ Tipperary,	94 1 10	153 11 5	
„ Limerick,	89 19 3	14 5 6	
	1,145 4 5	5,537 6 5	7,673 12 8

10. Sea and Coast Fisheries Loan Fund, 47 & 48 Vic., c. 93 :—
Repayments,
Dividends on Stock, &c.,   =   5,623 13 0 / 454 6 8   6,027 18 8

11. Galway Harbour Receiver's Account :—
Dues,
Sale of Engine, Materials, &c. ; Refunds,   =   3,792 19 2 / 183 10 3   3,976 9 5

12. Southern Railway :—
Net Revenue for year ending 31st December, 1890,   —   3,893 17 0
Amount incurred for payment of Baronial Guaranteed Dividends,   —   3,142 12 6   7,036 9 6

Carried forward,   —   —   50,705 17 0

of Public Works in the Year ended 31st March, 1891.

SERVICES—continued.

EXPENDITURE—continued.	£ s. d.	£ s. d.	£ s. d.
Brought forward,	—	—	15,681 8 2
8. Loftus Hall, 41 Vic., c. 1:—			
Rent and Salaries,	—	179 16 4	
Transfer to Her Majesty's Exchequer,	—	250 0 0	429 16 4

9. Irish Reproductive Loan Fund, 37 & 38 Vic., c. 86, &c.:—

	Purchase of Stock.			Advances.	Law Costs.	
	£ s. d.					
County Clare,	200 0 0			101 0 0	3 6 6	
„ Cork,	600 0 0			1,731 10 0	0 16 2	
„ Galway,	—			3,516 10 0	25 11 6	
„ Kerry,	100 0 0			1,165 0 0	5 19 9	
„ Leitrim,	100 0 0			—	—	
„ Mayo,	—			1,145 0 0	12 5 7	
„ Sligo,	—			171 0 0	3 10 9	
„ Roscommon,	200 0 0			—	—	
„ Tipperary,	900 0 0			309 0 0	—	
„ Limerick,	100 0 0			—	—	
	2,500 0 0			7,411 0 0	52 17 3	10,670 17 9

10. Sea and Coast Fisheries Loan Fund, 47 & 48 Vic., c. 21:—			
Loans to Fishermen,	—	1,822 0 0	
Law Costs and Agents' Commission for recovery of instalments in arrear,	—	31 13 3	
Purchase of Stock,	—	4,000 0 0	5,913 13 3

11. Galway Harbour Receipts Account:—			
Repayment of Loan,	—	3,190 8 0	
Salaries, Maintenance of Works, &c.,	—	520 16 6	4,811 5 9

12. Southern Railway:—			
Repayment of Interest on Loan,	—	1,300 0 0	
Rent and General Charges,	—	380 5 3	
Dividends on Baronial Guaranteed Stock,	—	5,145 0 0	5,833 5 3
Carried forward,	—	—	42,549 0 11

(A 7.)—An Account showing the Receipts and Expenditure of the Commissioners

MISCELLANEOUS

RECEIPTS—continued.	£ s. d.	£ s. d.	£ s. d.
Brought forward,			86,701 17 0
13. Government Railways:— Net Revenue for year ending 31st December, 1890,	—	—	6,112 0 0
14. Emigration Grants,	—	—	—
15. Sundry Accounts:—			
Curragh of Kildare,	—	17 13 5	
Lunacy Inspection,	—	604 19 10	
Income Tax,	—	611 2 3	
Land Commission (Church Property) Office,	—	400 0 0	
George Glenny—Labourers' Dwellings Loan, Bandon's Account,	—	125 0 0	
Repr. of Hugh Kelly— Do., do.,	—	467 19 7	
Guard Irvine— Do., do.,	—	87 0 0	
Clogher Valley Tramway,	—	6,150 0 0	
Cavan, Leitrim, and Roscommon Railway,	—	1,953 7 3	
Cork and Muskerry Railway,	—	12,417 16 9	
Builders' Deposits, lodged with Tenders,	—	48 0 0	
Dividends on Stock lodged as Contractors' security,	—	5 13 8	
Island Bridge Waterworks,	—		
Board of Admiralty,	—	13 19 9	
Board of Trade,	—	15 0 0	
Drainage Works, Owning Amount,	—	15 11 6	
Fishery Loan Funds, Stamps,	—	19 7 9	
Temporary Receipts,	—	11,455 10 7	35,448 4 0
			86,603 10 10

of Public Works in the year ended 31st March, 1891.
SERVICES—continued.

EXPENDITURE—continued.	£ s. d.	£ s. d.	£ s. d.
Brought forward,	—	—	60,543 0 11
13. LETTERKENNY RAILWAY :—			
Repayment of Interest on Loan,	=	1,900 0 0	
General Charges,	=	142 4 4	
			2,042 4 4
14. EMIGRATION GRANTS :—			
Grant to Scheduled Unions,	—	—	61 10 4
15. SUNDRY ACCOUNTS :—			
Borough of Kildare,	—	67 18 8	
Loans Insurance,	—	400 19 0	
Income Tax,	—	900 1 1	
Land Commission (Church Property) Office,	—	923 14 10	
Kinsale Harbour,	—	0 1 6	
George Chorley—Labourers Dwellings Loan, Receiver's Account,	—	129 6 8	
Repe. of Hugh Kelly— Do., do.,	—	448 18 8	
Gerard Irvine— Do., do.,		151 10 0	
Clogher Valley Tramway,	—	2,170 9 0	
Cavan, Leitrim, and Roscommon Railway,	—	1,962 7 8	
Cork and Muskerry Railway,	—	11,238 3 9	
Builders' Deposits, refunded,	—	40 0 0	
Dividends on Stock lodged as Commrs'. Security,	—	5 12 0	
Island Bridge Waterworks,	—	1 17 9	
Board of Admiralty,	—	10 1 9	
Board of Trade,	—	19 4 7	
Drumore Works Closing Account,	—	0 10 4	
Fishery Loan Fund Stamps,	—	12 4 4	
Temporary Receipts,	—	1,153 6 9	
			24,157 14 11
			48,520 17 19
Balance,	—	—	20,454 13 0
			69,957 10 19

F. L. WEBB, Accountant.

(A 8.)—ARTERIAL DRAINAGE.—

These Works are executed by District Boards in

SCHEDULE.—ABSTRACT of FINAL AWARDS, and Repayments

Names	Counties	Date when Awards made final.	Areas of Flooded or Injured Lands which have been Relieved or Improved by Drainage Works	Cost per Acre of the Drainage measured, &c.	Increase in the Annual Letting Value of those Lands caused by Drainage.	Amount of Instalment Annually paid or payable to repay Cost, including Annual Maintenance	
			a. r. p.	£ s. d.	£ s. d.	£ s. d.	

Abbey River	Meath	6th April, 1886					
Ballynacurra	Limerick	2nd Oct., 1873	170				
Ballyrahan	Queen's	9th Oct., 1845					
Ballynanrig	King's and Queen's	PO April, 1886					
Ballytaigue & Kilmore	Wexford	6th Oct., 1868					
Belmony	Kildare	18th Mar., 1873					
Bunmurry	Limerick	3rd April, 1882					
Cashloorrig	King's	17th Mar., 1873					
Brickey River	Waterford	26th Sept., 1878					
Bride River	Cork	9th Oct., 1882					
Camoge	Limerick	26th Sept., 1878					
Clodiagh River	Tipperary	20th May, 1875					
Cashen	Kerry	9th Oct., 1868					
Cannell	Kildare	18th Jan., 1876					
Currygrane	Longford	6th Oct., 1882					
Dernishagh	King's	6th Oct., 1874					
Dunbyle	Limerick	6th Oct., 1871					
Douglas River	Carlow	31st Mar., 1876					
Ophin	Roscommon	20th Mar., 1872					
Follistown	Meath	9th Oct., 1882					
Frankford River	King's	17th Mar., 1873					
Do.	Do.	6th April, 1884	—	—	—		
Garristown and Dublin	Meath and Dublin	3rd April, 1886					
Glashuee	Cork	6th April, 1886					
Greenagh	Limerick	6th April, 1886					
Gully	Queen's	6th Oct., 1873					
		Brought forward		—			

a These charges have expired.

£ s. d.	£ s. d.	£ s. d.	
15,790 8 3	447 10 9	13,798 4 3	Ashley River.
1,308 4 9	97 10 0	1,295 18 8	Ballinamony.
1,125 10 11	149 16 10	1,995 15 9	Ballydota.
8,608 14 11	903 16 9	8,803 9 0	Ballymartrig.
630 16 9	723 9 6	3,944 10 2	Ballynligun and Kilteran.
6,714 7 1	690 15 6	8,844 0 0	Baltraney.
3,513 19 10	449 11 6	2,893 10 10	Barnskyle.
430 10 10	89 0 9	439 11 6	
3,714 11 0	140 17 10	3,649 9 10	Barlinstrig.
5,535 3 11	259 0 0	5,412 10 7	Brickey River.
8,867 15 5	316 9 3	3,531 9 8	Bride River.
7,533 11 5	443 0 0	7,651 12 5	Cattage.
7,977 19 10	340 17 1	8,809 16 0	Clodiagh River.
—	13 9 1	13 9 5	Cashen
6,188 10 3	112 15 9	3,801 11 7	Cantell.
916 2 7	10 0 0	803 11 3	Carryyrara.
5,689 0 5	50 11 0	5,190 1 5	Castlelough.
1,943 1 8	49 7 6	6,941 5 0	Donkyle.
18,664 19 5	240 10 9	18,357 10 5	Dunglea River.
17,600 15 7	793 9 5	16,664 9 0	Elphin.
60 13 3	64 10 0	145 11 1	Felistoro
6,175 19 9	341 5 7	6,041 19 9	Freakford River
350 4 10	103 17 1	442 1 11	Do
8,737 19 10	588 14 4	8,890 15 3	Garystown and Dulea.
44 9 1	115 7 9	147 19 3	Glasheen
513 9 0	938 9 9	1,549 0 8	Greenagh.
4,909 19 7	169 1 9	6,999 15 6	Gully.

			£ s. d.	£ s. d.	£ s. d.	£ s. d.
		Carried forward, . . .	58,593 0 30	—	10,742 0 1	3,584 13 6
Gully Upper, . .	Queen's, . . .	14th Mar., 1670,	604 1 10	4 13 1	789 11 1	40 4 0
Hogan's Pass, . .	Tipperary, . .	9th Oct., 1678, .	614 1 20	5 19 0	205 19 10	191 1 3
Insy. Upper, . . {	Meath, Westmeath, Longford, & Cavan, }	4th April, 1691,	13,674 2 7	7 × 3	2,780 3 4	1,447 11 3
Island Lehan and } Glare River,	Mayo, . . .	2nd April, 1873,	1,617 8 37	4 16 4	413 5 6	168 15 10
Kildare, . .	Kildare, . . .	20th Sept., 1877,	2,047 9 35	2 11 4	806 7 10	{ 69 1 11 }
Kilmastalla, . .	Tipperary, . .	7th July, 1870,	1,601 1 18	6 10 7	541 17 2	{ 811 5 7 }
Lorton, . .	Meath, . . .	3rd April, 1680,	679 1 29	7 0 7	604 11 10	193 19 5
Lee River, . .	Kildare and Carlow, .	9th Oct., 1883, .	1,634 3 22	10 × 11	656 0 0	814 5 7
Lough Oughter, . .	Cavan, . . .	4th April, 1876,	2,577 1 60	4 4 11	448 10 9	209 14 8
Midford, . .	Cork, . . .	5th Oct., 1857, .	1,915 9 10	6 14 6	440 0 7	721 10 10
Morning Star, Upper,	Limerick, . .	6th April, 1888,	620 3 25	3 17 0	256 4 0	170 7 6
Mulkear River, . .	Limerick, . .	20th Sept., 1877,	4,320 2 24	9 4 1	972 9 11	385 17 9
Navvy River, . .	Meath, . .	4th April, 1884,	714 3 9	10 6 1	315 15 2	1100 19 6
Do. Upper, {	Do., . .	4th April, 1884,	102 1 10	6 1 9	72 11 9	90 1 10
Oarmmm, . .	Do., . . .	4th April, 1869,	2,387 2 0	3 0 9	601 1 9	278 0 11
Parsonstown, . .	Tipperary and King's,	28th Sept., 1674,	2,310 0 1	4 4 8	830 19 3	810 16 2
Quinagh, . .	Carlow, . .	30th Jan., 1678,	860 3 0	0 10 3	820 1 6	68 10 0
Rathangan River, .	Kildare, . .	4th April, 1863,	8,964 × 3	9 10 6	5,094 10 10	1,334 13 10
Rathdowney, . .	Queen's, . .	5th Oct., 2829,	412 1 80	6 4 1	189 6 6	26 6 9
River River, .	King's & Westmeath,	5th Oct., 1873,	1,472 1 30	6 19 9	915 10 9	{ 99 1 11 }
Rambridge, . .	Clare, . .	4th April, 1871,	2,368 9 4	7 15 2	1,229 14 11	{ 410 15 8 }
Sunnyford River, .	Kildare, . .	9th Oct., 1804, .	3,694 0 6	6 18 3	1,455 13 10	577 9 16
Sunnlinher, .	Cavan, . . .	23rd Mar., 1869,	695 9 10	7 6 5	143 15 7	59 9 8
Swilly Burn, . .	Donegal, . .	9th Oct., 1896,	1,404 2 19	6 3 1	443 9 5	115 5 10
Turret River, . .	Tyrone, . .	3rd April, 1874,	453 1 14	11 7 1	330 10 10	{ 104 9 8 }
Tory Hill, . .	Limerick, . .	3rd April, 1872,	691 1 2	4 4 6	484 13 4	{ 110 2 6 }
Trassery, . .	Cork, . .	5th Sept., 1880,	500 0 17	6 9 9	945 16 4	{ 50 14 6 } { 20 37 10 }
Ward River, . .	Dublin and Meath,	4th April, 1863,	920 0 16	7 16 1	514 7 5	163 19 0
(Continued to next page.)		Total, .	21,413 3 19	4 1 6	72,556 14 31	19,529 7 6

26 & 27 Vic., c. 88, &c.

accordance with the Provisions of the above Act.
thereon, for the Year ended 31st March, 1891.

Total Amount Advanced, including balances in time of Arrear.	Portion of Total Advances charged to Counties for Public Works or ordered by Drainage Board.	Amount charged on Lands.	Repayments			Remarks.
			To end of year, 1890.	For year ended 31st March, 1891.	Total.	
£ s. d.	£ s. d.	£ s. d.	£ s. d.	£ s. d.	£ s. d.	
{ 163,217 11 1	8,457 11 0	108,586 68 5	117,283 11 11	8,240 15 3	125,733 0 4	
77,516 0 0 }						
2,447 13 9	70 0 0	2,527 13 9	1,261 11 9	89 4 11	1,848 15 1	Bully, Upper.
4,146 16 0	{ 914 4 0	4,912 8 0	1,172 8 8	941 4 4	1,448 7 8	Rogue's Pass,
	+228 0 0 }					
62,094 3 0	{ 8,193 13 5	64,573 12 0	41,519 16 10	6,064 19 0	67,676 18 1	Inny, Upper.
	+2,724 0 0 }					
8,704 13 7	{ 912 8 5	8,540 18 7	4,188 14 3	290 7 10	4,448 6 0	{ Island Lakes and Glore
	+124 0 0 }					River.
8,857 4 0	900 0 0	8,377 1 0	5,886 0 0	900 1 0	6,786 0 0	Kildare
10,680 7 0	—	10,580 7 0	11,587 13 5	925 16 1	14,193 10 6	Kilcomalia
6,817 19 10	81 14 1	4,181 17 0	2,872 16 9	450 0 9	3,154 4 11	Larana.
87,816 9 9	794 6 0	87,714 9 0	5,865 11 9	1,134 4 9	6,889 16 6	Lee River.
18,184 6 0	—	18,184 4 0	7,849 2 9	1,068 19 0	10,416 1 7	Lough Oughter.
6,871 14 4	—	8,831 12 0	854 16 9	842 19 0	1,897 9 3	Milford.
7,863 0 0	620 0 0	7,173 0 0	770 0 0	347 10 0	1,168 0 0	Morning Star, Upper
38,778 9 9	884 1 0	19,914 10 0	16,788 6 11	1,533 8 0	19,588 15 0	McPheer River.
8,582 6 7	{ 544 6 0	8,048 6 0	1,287 11 0	803 19 0	1,691 11 3	Nanny River.
	+94 19 7 }					
1,843 18 0	—	1,843 18 0	75 6 5	60 3 5	130 9 8	Do. Upper
11,485 18 6	348 14 5	11,181 10 0	1,178 1 10	445 0 7	4,723 8 6	Owenton
11,689 17 1	128 0 0	31,546 17 1	8,249 11 0	688 48 7	9,033 6 3	Forematotio.
2,706 18 9	790 0 0	1,909 18 0	3,491 8 5	135 1 0	4,667 9 1	Quinagh
77,802 6 9	4,145 0 9	70,889 6 9	27,383 19 9	0,478 4 1	44,044 77 9	Enimnegan River.
2,545 9 2	—	2,446 0 5	5,606 5 0	88 0 5	5,726 14 9	Kathinreagh.
5,971 9 9	—	5,871 9 9	4,004 6 5	198 9 10	4,598 10 9	Silver River.
28,989 12 11	481 1 0	18,904 28 5	22,381 13 9	710 9 5	14,637 7 5	Kambibridge.
18,226 0 0	{ 1,846 11 10	30,984 0 5	18,481 18 0	1,143 7 10	11,693 1 90	Saneyford River.
	+083 0 0 }					
2,683 3 9	765 0 0	1,900 6 5	1,288 19 8	81 18 0	1,440 17 9	Bromflabat
9,526 18 5	{ 497 14 0	8,857 14 0	3,865 79 7	881 9 0	4,785 8 7	Softly Sun
	+14 4 8 }					
4,592 1 0	167 10 0	4,164 11 9	5,177 0 9	176 48 90	3,588 17 0	Torrent River.
8,110 18 9	—	8,110 18 9	4,318 14 4	176 17 9	4,391 12 1	Tory Hill.
9,483 16 0	78 9 0	1,083 16 0	—	131 8 9	131 8 9	Trastura.
4,863 17 9	196 19 0	4,641 19 9	2,582 13 1	944 19 4	2,587 16 9	Ward River.

(A 8.)—ARTERIAL DRAINAGE.—

These Works are executed by District Boards in

ARTERIAL DRAINAGE WORKS in progress

District.	Counties.	Date when Awards made final.	Area of Flooded or Injured Lands, which have been Drained or Improved, Maintained in Mature Manner.	Cost per Acre of the Drainage, including Arterial, &c.	Increase in the Annual Letting Value of these Lands, caused by Drainage.	Amount of Instalments payable per Annum, to repay Cost and Interest, after deducting the Redemptions.	
			A. R. P.	£ s. d.	£ s. d.	£ s. d.	
	From preceding page,	"	—	—	—	12,339 7	
Ballynahinch, . .	Tipperary . .	"	—	—	—	—	
Fullmort, . . .	Meath . . .	"	—	—	—	—	
Kilbeg, . . .	Cork, . .	"	—	—	—	—	
Lough Erne, . .	Fermanagh, Cavan, Monaghan, and Donegal.	"	—	—	—	—	
Do. (Navigation),	Do. . .	"	—	—	—	430 4 10	
Deer Park, . . .	—	"	—	—	—	—	
	Total charge against districts,		—	—	—	12,339 15 5	

Office of Public Works, Dublin, 1st May, 1891.

26 & 27 Vic., c. 68, &c.

accordance with the Provisions of the above Acts.

showing the Loans made to 31st March, 1891.

Total Amount advanced including re-payment Interest to date of Award.	Portion of Total Advance charged as Counties for Public Works, or refunded by Postage Board.	Amount charged on Lands.	Repayments		
			To this Month last	For year ended 31st March, 1891.	Total.

APPENDIX B

Return of the Number of Vessels and Amount of Tonnage that have entered at Kamehdt Harbour during the Year 1890-91.

Month																			
April																			
May																			
June																			
July																			
August																			
September																			
October																			
November																			
December																			
January																			
February																			
March																			

F. H. Chapman, General Manager

KINGSTOWN HARBOUR.

SUMMARY of RAINFALL and TIDAL OBSERVATIONS.

Month.	Fall in Inches.	Thermometer in Fahrenheit's Booth.		Barometer Number of Days on Which Rain Fell.	Measurement at High Water.			Measurement at Low Water.		
		Max.	Min.		Mean.	Height.	Wind.	Mean.	Height.	Wind.
1890.					ft. in.			ft. in.		
April,	1·17	46	37	11	12	13 2	W.	16	-0 2	E.
May,	1·45	8	39	15	7	12 4	S.S.E.	5	+0 6	S.W.
June,	1·70	3	24	17	5	12 3	W.	7	—	N.E.
July,	1·11	70	50	10	9	13 0	W.W.W.	3	-0 1	W.S.W.
August,	1·17	60	62	13	20	14 5	N.E.	6	-0 2	W.
September,	1·90	31	42	7	3	12 5	W.S.W.	1	-0 6	R.W.
October,	3·5	1	36	9	1	12 5	N.W.	6	—	N.W.
November,	4·52	11	28	20	10	12 1	S.E.	11	+0 6	N.E.
December,	5·74	3	12	8	13	12 9	S.W.	11	+1 5	N.W.
1891.										
January,	·57	51	25	8	21	12 6	S.E.	16	—	N.W.
February,	·47	52	47	1	11	13 9	N.W.	5	-0 6	S.W.
March,	·74	19	43	0	14	13 9	E.N.E.	15	-0 1	N.N.E.

THE RETURN of Fish landed from Trawlers and Herring Boats from 1st April, 1890, to 31st March, 1891.

	Trawl fish.	Shell fish.	Summer Herrings.	Winter Herrings.
	Number of Hampers.	Number of Hampers.	Mease and Hundreds.	Mease and Hundreds.
1890.				
April,	113½	—	—	—
May,	1,731½	—	—	—
June,	819	—	—	—
July,	1,167	—	—	—
August,	1,744	—	—	—
September,	2,116	—	—	—
October,	1,684	—	—	—
November,	1,353	—	—	—
December,	660	—	—	—
1891.				
January,	1,063	—	—	—
February,	277	—	—	—
March,	1,419	652½	163·9½	88·3½
Total,	13,892	652½	163·9½	88·3½

Average prices for the year for trawl fish would be about £1 10s., and for herrings, £1 6s. per mease; shell fish, 17s. 6d. per hamper.

The trawl fishing was above the average, showing an increase of about 3,000 hampers landed over the previous season; the number of boats fishing being about the same, viz., average 52 boats of from 40 to 60 tons each.

The season was favourable for trawling.

There was a strike by the crews of these vessels for more wages and better allowances, in which they were not successful; it lasted for six weeks, including the month of February, and accounts for the small quantity landed at that time.

The amount of shell fish landed was up to the average, obtained entirely by the trawlers; there is no pot fishing done here.

The herring fishing was a failure, about 24 Scotch and 8 Arklow boats only getting 163 mease during the summer. In the winter only the local boats fished, and although they persevered fishing every opportunity, they only succeeded in landing 88 mease.

Howth Harbour.—County Dublin.

The herring fishing for the past year at Howth is still on the decline. One boat fished from 6th to 26th of May, but caught nothing; from the 26th of May there were several boats fishing until the 5th of July, and the average price was good (viz.: £1 12s. 8d.), but the quantity was not at all equal to former years, and most of the Scotch boats left, but the local boats did well until the end of July. The number of fishing boats during the herring season were as follows—Scotch, 40; Irish, 53; Manx 2; total 95.

The number of mease of herrings taken was 8,836, and sold at an average price of 16s.

There was a splendid market for book fish; 221,173 having been sold and realised the sum of £10,684.

The vessels having been reclassed for tonnage makes a great decrease in the amount received for harbour dues.

The imports for year were as follows :—

Coal, 3,556 tons.
Fish, 2,013 barrels of oysters.

Dunmore Harbour.—County Waterford

Within the past year we had 29 large cutters trawling in the deep out of Dunmore, the takes of the higher class of head fish, such as sole, turbot, brit, and dorse, have fallen off, but prices are higher, and ranged as follows: sole, 12d.; turbot, 9d.; brot and dorse, 3d. per lb.; cod and hake, which were so plentiful in past seasons have been very scarce nothing but complaints are heard among the sailing trawl fishermen; they ascribe the scarcity to the large fleet of steam trawlers fishing off here for the last three years; they are increasing year after year; several of them put into here for shelter; but do not sell their fish, they bring it to other ports; principally to Liverpool and Milford, where they get a better market.

The herring fishing commenced on the 1st July; only a few mease captured until the 10th October; from that date the takes improved, but we had not the means of catching them, as the large boats were at the western ports, fishing mackarel, and could not leave on account of being engaged for the season at 10s. a hundred, and £30 as a premium; on the 1st November, the weather broke and as usual the herrings took their departure from here up the north channel.

The salmon fishing in the lower waters of the river Suir and Barrow is this year below the average; complaints about the scarcity are also heard among the drift net fishermen. The price of salmon has ranged between 2s. 6d. and 1s. 11d. per lb.; at the present it is at 1s. 11d.

The shell fishermen that ply their calling off these coasts, are the only fishermen that did well during the past season; takes were good and prices fair. Lobsters, 12s. to 10s.; crabs, 2s. to 2s. 6d. per dozen.

The quantity of fish sold at Dunmore was—herrings 1,320 mease, average 14s. 8d. a mease; all other fish, 8,251 cwt. at £4,265 10s. The number of boats employed were as follows: herring boats, Irish, 53; trawlers, English, 15; Irish, 14; lobster boats, Irish, 6; making a total of 88 boats—1,162 tons; 558 men; cargo vessels, 14—1,039, tons, 65 men.

Imports were :—Coal, 1,641 tons; salt, 30 tons.

Donaghadee Harbour.—County Down.

There have been two cases of stranding in the harbour during the year, both caused to the collier, "Kitty Clyde" of Belfast, a regular trader to this port, and caused by the mismanagement of those on board, who did not anchor in sufficient time to bring her to in her usual berth, and also using defective warps; on both occasions the vessel received no damage.

Three vessels arrived in the harbour in distress, were beached, and received temporary repairs, enabling them to proceed to their destination.

The import of coal has increased 169 tons, viz., from 16,042 in 1890, to 16,212 in 1891.

In the month of June, 12 fishing vessels owned by Messrs. Corrin, Brothers, Isle of Man, arrived for a week's trial of the herring fishery off this port, intending, should the week's trial prove a success, to establish a fishing depot there. On the first night's trial, the average capture being only one mease each boat, they decided to abandon further trial and bore up for home.

Fourteen Manx, 3 Scotch, and 7 Irish fishing vessels took shelter in the harbour during the year. The cod fishing season has now closed at this port, and has proved a successful one, the fish plentiful, of good marketable quality and sold at prices ranging from £1 per dozen at the commencement, to 15s. per dozen at the close.
Other small branches of fishery at this port have been a total failure.

A RETURN showing the Harbour Service for the Twelve Months ending the 31st March, 1891.

	Vessels	Tons
Shipping—Tonnage entering the Harbour with Cargoes to discharge—or load,	104	8,681
Tonnage resorting to the Harbour for shelter,	55	2,850
Number of Tons of Coal imported,	—	15,812

Other Merchandise, Imported and Exported:—

IMPORTED			EXPORTED		
	Tons			Tons	
Salt Fish,	12		Scrap Iron,	15	
Granite,	108		Potatoes,	68	
			Brick,	43,020	

	Vessels	Tons	Men
Number of Fishing Vessels resorting to the Harbour for Shelter, with their Tonnage and Number of Men,	20	440	188

	Boxes	£	s.	d.
Quantity of Herrings landed and sold, and price sold at,	193	107	2	6

	Tug Boats	Yachts
Number of Tug Boats and Yachts using the Harbour,	44	40

TABLE showing the Number of Vessels of all kinds that arrived in Harbour during the year ending 31st March, 1891.

—	Registered Tonnage	Cargo Tonnage	Description of Cargo	Observations
101 Sailing Vessels,	8,682	15,812	Coal,	Discharged cargo.
8 ,, ,,	178	—	Bricks,	Taking in cargo, 3,360 bricks.
1 ,, ,,	94	94	Potatoes and scrap iron,	Taking in cargo.
44 Tug Steamers,	—	—	—	Called into harbour either for shelter or for orders.
60 Coasting Vessels,	—	—	—	Called into harbour for shelter.
20 Fishing Boats,	—	—	—	Do., do.
40 Yachts,	—	—	—	Called into harbour either for shelter or for orders.
11 Fishing Boats,	—	—	Herrings,	To sell.

ARDGLASS HARBOUR.

Fishing commenced here on 26th May, which was a few days before the usual time, and it ended on 25th September, about three weeks before the usual time. The capture of herrings all through the season was very small, indeed it may be said the fishing at this station was almost a failure. The total number of boats engaged equals 219, or 6 more than the season before; but the quantity of fish captured was little over one-third of the quantity mentioned in last Report, viz., 17,349 mease, against 6,522 this last season. During all last season the demand was good, and the prices ranged from 37s. 6d. down to 4s. per mease, the average all through equal to 19s. per mease, which was the highest average for many years past.

Only two steamers called here for herrings during the entire season, and both had to leave without them.

Fishing boats here last season :—63 Scotch, 51 Manx, 105 Irish. Total, 219.

Out of the above number about 75 boats called here with fish from one to six times, and the remainder fished from here nearly all the season.

I

Table showing the Number of Vessels of all kinds trading during the year, either to Discharge or take in Cargo.

—	Registered Tonnage	Cargo Tonnage	Description of Cargo	Observations
11 Sailing Vessels,	774	1,543	Coal,	Discharged cargo.
7 " "	419	444	Potatoes,	Taking in cargo.
7 Steamers,	784	1,038	Do.,	Do.
2 Sailing Vessels,	111	150	Salt,	Discharging cargo.
1 Smack,	29	24	Oats,	Taking in cargo.
8 Steamers,	135	—	Herrings,	Called and had to leave without them.
4 Smacks,	30	—	Do.,	Do. do. do.

Note.—In addition to the above, twenty-eight Tug Boats called here Harbour during the year, either for shelter or for orders, and ten Trading Vessels called for shelter.

APPENDIX C.

REPORT ON ANCIENT MONUMENTS.

CAHERS, RATH-ACTIVILLAGES and BEEHIVE STRUCTURES on the Promontory of Dingle.

There are few parts of Ireland of greater historical interest than Dingle. An ancient Spanish settlement from the earliest period, here a considerable Spanish trade was carried on by settlers, which lasted to the time of Elizabeth. The early name of the place was Daingean-hi-chuis, translated the fortress of Cuis—the Irish proprietor before the English invasion. The modern name, Dingle-i-Couch, is a corruption of the former. The Husseys, the Desmonds, and Ormonds, all held sway in the district, and finally Fitzgerald, Knight of Kerry. A charter was granted by Elizabeth, but not confirmed until the fourth year of James I. Some centuries before our era the great Milesian expedition from Spain landed in this part of Ireland; and to this remote period we attribute the wonderful collection of prehistoric remains which have lately been scheduled under the protection of the Ancient Monuments Act, and which I have only partially been able to inspect.

The whole promontory of Corkaguiny is rich in remains of great interest to the antiquary.

In the Archæological Proceedings of Kilkenny of 1858 will be found a most interesting article by Richard Hitchcock, entitled "Dingle in the Sixteenth Century," in which he gives a list of ruins which existed in his day; how many of these now survive it is impossible to say, but that the whole country presents objects of great interest is undoubted. In former days this now thinly inhabited district must have had a considerable population; it has been the battlefield of contending parties, down to the Desmond men of the sixteenth century, and tradition points to great battles being fought in the vicinity at the earliest times.

In mentioning these reputed battles I repeat a statement which has been frequently made to me, with some evidence of truth, that in the bog near Brandon, where one of these great battles was fought, numbers of arrows are still picked up. I have seen some of these rude implements, which certainly have been shaped into pointed forms and may have been used as bolts; on the other hand, Mr. Darcy of Dingle, who takes the deepest interest in its antiquities, tells me that he has found numbers of these arrows, and that he has seen them between two and three feet long, and that they had a notch for the bowstring.

Taking a circuit from Dingle in the direction of Smerwick, we come first to the cemetery of Gariffnuy and Ballintaggart. The first has no remains of the ancient church, but two monuments are worthy of notice: a head stone with the inscription thereon, the other a rude carving of Christ on the cross, with indications of metal attachments, such as the nails in the feet and pins which held the crown of thorns.

At Ballintaggart there is nothing save a surrounding moat and several Ogham stones. The cemetery of Dingle Church contains monuments of great interest.

Kilmakedar Church, the oratory of Gallarus, the eidne circles and cloughauns together with Gallarus Castle, have been carefully preserved from ruin under the provisions of the Church Act.

Following the road along the coast we come to Smerwick and Ferriters Cove, and further on Dunquins and the village of Coumeenoole.

The roads from Dunquinn and from Dingle by Slea Head here nearly meet, but there is an interval of about two hundred yards over which the car has to be carried; if this missing link were completed the drive would be one of the finest in Ireland. On the hills near Commeenoole are numbers of ancient dwellings, some below the ground and others above, some enclosed within stone cashels. It is almost impossible to do more to these rude structures beyond the replacing of a few stones which have fallen in and that a careful examination of the soil of the interior should be made with a view to finding any objects of interest.

Leaving Commeenoole, we follow the road along the coast with a magnificent view of the Blasquets, meaning "cut off rocks." On these islands are similar structures to those at Commeenoole: on Inishnabro are underground chambers; on Inishvickelane there is an oratory; on Inishtooskert I hear there are many dwellings of this sort, but it is impossible, without waiting for days, to effect a landing on this island, which is fertile, and good grazing ground, but the difficulty of landing, or when you have landed, getting off, prevents any attempt at occupation. It is certainly most singular that in so many parts of the world the love of isolation appears to have affected man. In these remote islands off the Irish coast the home of the recluse is to be found. In High Island, The Blasquets, The Skellig, and numberless other places, the hermit or the monk must have been left to his own devices for procuring food, or must have lived on the charity of the faithful.

Driving towards Dingle, the Ordnance map indicates where numbers of these cells similar to those at Commeenoole exist, but the rugged nature of the mountain side precludes the possibility of more extended examination. It would take a very considerable time to make a report on the objects of interest in this locality, which can only be done by degrees. A few miles from Commeenoole brings us to the fort of Dunbeg, with its lines of fortifications and curious construction.

As on the Arran islands, this fort appears to have been constructed as a defence from a land force. There are four lines of circumvallation, with indications of a passage from the sea side to the last line of defence. I am greatly disposed to think that this fort was erected as a protection to a shrine which stands on the plateau near the sea, as indicated in plan; round this cell are indications of a stone circle, but it is impossible to arrive at a clear conclusion until an exhaustive examination of this building is made.

Near Dunbeg are many more stone-roofed cells, but in a very ruinous condition.

About a quarter of a mile in the Dingle direction is the fort, as indicated by the annexed tracing. The wall is very perfect, and I have no doubt that a careful examination of this building will prove of interest.

Further on are several fine pillar stones and earthen forts. I have in this report only indicated a few of the objects of archæological interest, and leave its completion to a time when it can be extended by the result of work that I hope to carry out.

What I suggest with regard to these monuments is as follows:—

1st.—That the Fort of Dunbeg be carefully examined, and that the chambers be cleared out; that the fallen stones be replaced, and the underground passage opened.

2nd.—That the Fort and Cloghauns near Dingle be treated in the same way, and that some further works be carried out at Commeenoole.

THOS. N. DEANE,
Superintendent.

TOWER OF LUSK.

This most peculiar tower stands at the western end of the Church of Lusk, the date of its erection is recorded in an old missal at Lusk Church, noted in the margin thus:—

"EGO ANNO EDIFICATUM FUIT CAMPANELLA NOVUM, 1480."

The existence of a round tower in the vicinity of a more ancient church led to its incorporation with the tower of 1480. The plan is square, with crenelated battlements and three 15th century towers at the corners, the fourth being the ancient round tower. There is a vaulted crypt beneath the ground. The walls and battlements have been pointed and the arch of the crypt concreted. Two interesting monuments, which were exposed to the weather in the graveyard, have been removed to the tower. All that is requisite for the protection of this building is being done.

I 2

APPENDIX

TRAMWAYS AND PUBLIC COMPANIES (IRELAND)

GENERAL STATISTICAL RETURN showing INCIDENCE of TAXATION on the several (Ireland) Act, 1883;

RAILWAY.	Co---.	State of Court in Second	Local Charges		Area Charged	
			Capital	Per Cent.	Designation.	Valuation.

D.

Act, 1883, 46 & 47 Vic., cap. 43.

Areas charged under Guarantees in pursuance of the Tramways and Public Companies 46 & 47 Vic., cap. 43.

[illegible]			[illegible]	[illegible]			[illegible]
[illegible]	[illegible]	[illegible]		[illegible]	[illegible]	[illegible]	
£ s. d.	£ s. d.	£ s. d.		£ s. d.	£ s. d.	£ s. d.	£ s. d.
[illegible]	[illegible]	[illegible]	[illegible]	[illegible]	[illegible]	[illegible]	[illegible]
[illegible]	[illegible]	[illegible]	[illegible]	[illegible]	[illegible]	[illegible]	[illegible]
[illegible]	[illegible]	[illegible]	[illegible]	[illegible]	[illegible]	[illegible]	[illegible]
[illegible]	[illegible]	[illegible]	[illegible]	[illegible]	[illegible]	[illegible]	[illegible]
[illegible]	[illegible]	[illegible]	[illegible]	[illegible]	[illegible]	[illegible]	[illegible]
[illegible]	[illegible]	[illegible]	[illegible]	—	—	—	—
[illegible]	[illegible]	[illegible]	[illegible]	—	—	—	—
[illegible]	[illegible]	[illegible]	[illegible]	[illegible]	[illegible]	[illegible]	[illegible]
[illegible]	[illegible]	[illegible]	[illegible]	[illegible]	[illegible]	[illegible]	[illegible]
[illegible]	[illegible]	[illegible]	[illegible]	[illegible]	[illegible]	[illegible]	[illegible]
[illegible]	[illegible]	[illegible]	[illegible]	[illegible]	[illegible]	[illegible]	[illegible]
[illegible]	[illegible]	[illegible]	[illegible]	[illegible]	[illegible]	[illegible]	[illegible]
[illegible]	[illegible]	[illegible]	[illegible]	—	—	—	—
[illegible]	[illegible]	[illegible]	[illegible]	—	—	—	—
—	—	—	—	—	—	—	—
[illegible]	[illegible]	[illegible]	[illegible]	—	—	—	—
—	—	—	—	—	—	—	—
—	—	—	—	—	—	—	—
—	—	—	—	[illegible]	[illegible]	[illegible]	[illegible]

APPENDIX K.

Seed Potatoes Supply (Ireland) Act, 1890, 54 Vic., c. 1.

APPENDIX F.

LIST OF PIERS AND HARBOURS NUMERICALLY ARRANGED COMMENCING WITH
COUNTY DUBLIN AND MARKED ON MAP.

No.	Name	County	No.	Name	County	No.	Name	County

DUBLIN : Printed for Her Majesty's Stationery Office,
By ALEX. THOM & Co. (Limited), 87, 88, & 89, Abbey-street.
The Queen's Printing Office.

Clougheun near Dunbeg

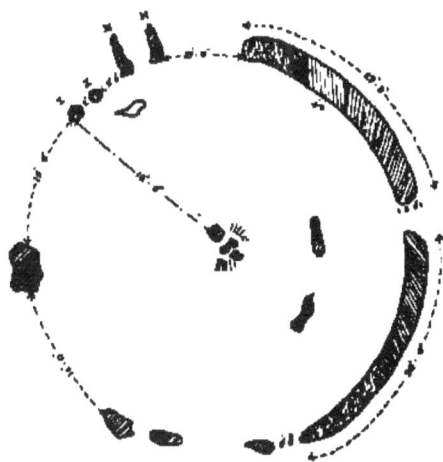

Z. Upright Stones.
X. Flat   do.

open

Covered

open

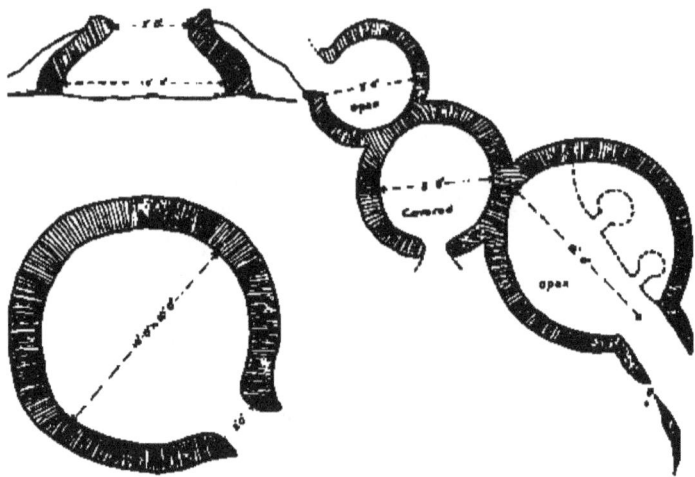

Walls very perfect, about
7'0" to 8'0" high.

Covered cell
about 6'0" high

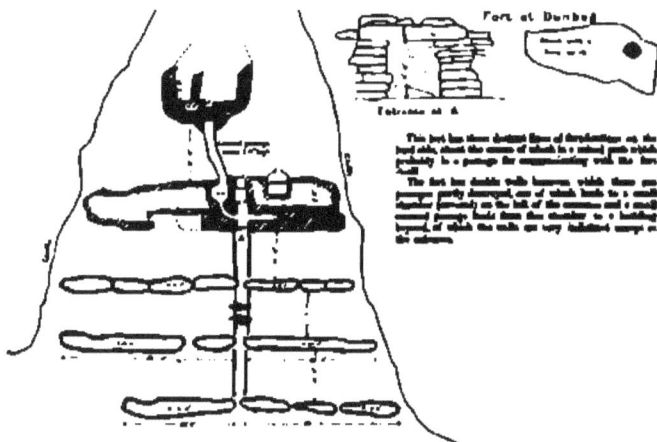

Fort at Dunbeg

Entrance at A.

This fort has three distinct lines of fortification on the land side, about the centre of which is a raised path which probably is a passage for communicating with the fort directly.

The fort has double walls however, which these outer ones partly destroyed, of which little to be properly traced, but from the entrance and occupation, which is little [illegible] the outer as a building the others.

www.ingramcontent.com/pod-product-compliance
Lightning Source LLC
Chambersburg PA
CBHW021527270326
41930CB00008B/1127